IMAGES
of America

UNITED STATES NAVAL TRAINING CENTER, BAINBRIDGE

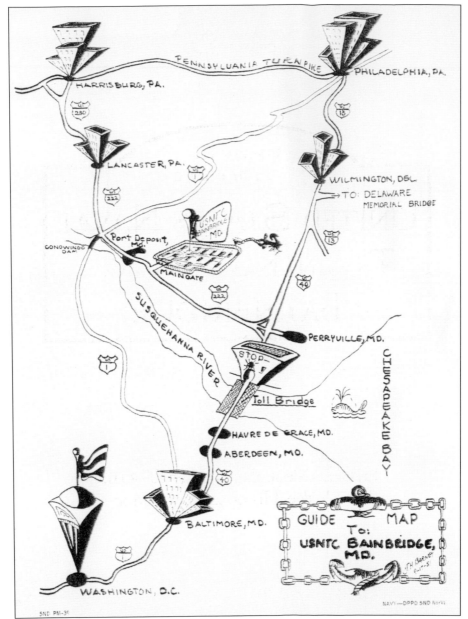

MAP OF BAINBRIDGE, 1951. This hand-drawn map to USNTC Bainbridge was created in 1951 and was used in informational brochures on base as well as in publications promoting Cecil County, Maryland, to emphasize both the location of the county and of towns such as Perryville and Port Deposit, as shown, as well as the ease with which one could travel to Bainbridge—even prior to the creation of I-95 and the Tydings Memorial Bridge. (Courtesy of Mike Miklas.)

ON THE COVER: Bainbridge Naval Training Center sits on a 300-foot cliff surrounded by farmland with the town of Port Deposit between it and the Susquehanna River, seemingly an odd location for a navy base. Yet hikes down the cliff to the river where whaleboats awaited remedied the situation of a landlocked navy base. (Department of the Navy, Naval Historical Center.)

IMAGES
of America

UNITED STATES NAVAL TRAINING CENTER, BAINBRIDGE

Erika L. Quesenbery on behalf of the
Bainbridge Historical Association

ARCADIA
PUBLISHING

Published by Arcadia Publishing
Charleston SC, Chicago IL, Portsmouth NH, San Francisco CA

Printed in the United States of America

Library of Congress Catalog Card Number: 2007921337

For all general information contact Arcadia Publishing at:
Telephone 843-853-2070
Fax 843-853-0044
E-mail sales@arcadiapublishing.com
For customer service and orders:
Toll-Free 1-888-313-2665

Visit us on the Internet at www.arcadiapublishing.com

*This book is dedicated to the honor and memory of the men and women
who served so proudly and so well at USNTC Bainbridge,
and those civilian men and women who worked on base,
all of whom are now the caretakers of its memories, stories, and history.*

CONTENTS

ACKNOWLEDGMENTS

This book could not have become reality without the archives of the Paw Paw Museum and NTC Bainbridge Museum, operated by Port Deposit Heritage Corporation and the NTC Bainbridge Historical Association, respectively. The men and women who volunteer for these organizations and preserve our shared past are owed a debt of gratitude that can never be fully repaid.

I owe a debt of appreciation and gratitude, as well, to Lauren Bobier, my editor at Arcadia Publishing, for believing in its work and for the motivation and guidance she provided from start to deadline.

Special gratitude and appreciation is extended to the men, women, and children who donated their time and energy (and intolerance to poison ivy) from 1997 to 2000 as the Tome School Clean-Up Volunteers on Bainbridge. Singled out among these many dedicated individuals are Capt. Jeff Borowy of the U.S. Navy, the last commander at Bainbridge; the Navy Seabees; Judge Walter Buck for sharing his memories with volunteers; Port Deposit Heritage Corporation; and Delegate David Rudolph, who founded the cleanup efforts.

To my parents, L. Ray and R. Ann Quesenbery, for their belief in me and for supporting my desires to write and record local history and to my husband, Kevin Matthews, for his unflagging support and patience.

Lastly and most especially, this book is dedicated to one sailor in particular who served at Bainbridge and met his beautiful bride there, Michael Miklas, president of the Bainbridge Historical Association in 2006–2007. Thank you, Mike, for keeping the memory of Bainbridge alive, for which you have become my hero.

INTRODUCTION

As difficult as it may be to imagine, if one didn't know about NTC Bainbridge and where it was situated in Cecil County, the 1,200-acre base could be passed by without a glance or notice. It is as if the base vanished or was a figment of thousands of imaginations, so little of it exists today. Sailors, WAVES (Women Accepted for Volunteer Service), and civilian workers from the base have returned in recent years for one last glimpse or to show their descendants the place where they slogged through mud or bunked with lifelong friends, only to stop at C. M. Tugs Restaurant in Port Deposit, or other venues, and inquire where they made a wrong turn. In the restaurant, proprietors John and Kathy Leeds understand the confusion and have a sort of shrine to Bainbridge with a model ship and old, dog-eared photograph collages hanging on the wall. They sit, coffee in hand, and explain that the base is atop the hill and tell the abbreviated story of Bainbridge.

The base is now covered in scrub trees, weeds, and brush and is littered with cast-off concrete boulders, crumbling sign monuments with ghostly lettering, and a few dozen derelict buildings determined to fight the elements and neglect to survive one more decade. The place is surrounded by a chain-link fence, an occasional rusted and fading sign warning, "No Trespassing, Federal Property," the only visible reminder from the road that there was once life here abundantly.

One must look beyond the crumbling facade and overgrown state of the massive tract of land. Looking at the surface, as it were, does not in any way tell the tale of the service of Bainbridge.

Built in 1942 during a crash program to provide wartime training facilities for 25,000 men and women, Bainbridge at its peak in 1945 had a total population of 38,000 personnel. It was the second of three naval recruit-training stations created from the same congressional appropriation in 1942, following the bombing of Pearl Harbor. Never meant for long service, the buildings were hastily constructed and meant to be temporary, but through periods of disuse or caretaker status, the base would be activated on and off through the early 1970s.

The base was named in honor of Commodore William Bainbridge after the financially lagging Tome School for Boys campus had been acquired through rather inspired maneuvering on the part of the school's board of trustees with the federal government and with interested army and navy inspectors, who were pitted against one another. Then over 50 farms and properties were acquired to make the over 1,000-acre base before, on May 7, 1942, the first crew of workmen from Charles H. Thompkins Company of Washington, D.C., arrived to begin construction of a navy base.

These crews, literally thousands of workers, descended on the towns of Port Deposit, Perryville, and Rising Sun and even on the nearby villages of Blythedale, Aikin, and Colora for housing as they built the base. Older homes became boarding houses, some housing men dormitory style in dining rooms and parlors, all contributing to the war effort. Leaflets were dropped out of planes in the southern United States calling for more workers. They came in droves, and the base took shape.

Four camps were built, each having a massive drill hall, drill field (or grinder), barracks, and other support structures. It took the work crews about two weeks to build a barracks with endless rows of bunks and lockers. Building the drill halls, with indoor pools for training purposes, took longer—about six months—and cost $1 million each. It took 15,000 men from all over the eastern United States, North and South, to build the gargantuan base, which cost some $50 million in the aggregate. But they achieved the impossible, and within four months, the first recruit was welcomed aboard NTC Bainbridge, even while construction activities continued.

After the arrival and hearty welcome of 19-year-old Damon Sutton from Pittsburgh, Pennsylvania, as the first recruit, more fresh-faced young men arrived in buses from the train station in nearby Aikin or Perryville. They passed by the guard box, where drivers were warned to dim their lights, and made their way to the processing center and on to one of the four regiments. Each regimental area, or camp, could house and train 5,000 men, and each camp functioned independently with a mess hall, barracks, drill hall, grinder, classrooms, rifle range, recreational facilities, and ships-service buildings.

By 1943, if the recruit was fortunate, he may have a chance to be a part of the physical-instructors program at Bainbridge. He would be lucky, because in May of that year, Comdr. Gene Tunny, the boxer, was in charge of this program. Commander Tunny expanded this program, which had been transferred from Norfolk, Virginia, into one that included such competitive sports as baseball and football, with the men playing in uniforms emblazoned with the team name of Commodores.

After World War II, the base was reduced to caretaker status, but on February 1, 1951, it was reactivated to meet demands of the Korean War. The first recruits arrived April 5, 1951, about 500 to 1,000 each week, with the first 500 recruits graduating from their 11-week training program on June 23, 1951. The base had four commands at this point—Service School, Recruit Training, U.S. Naval Hospital, and Administrative. The last of these commands was responsible for security, supply, maintenance, communication, and even medical care for the some 25,000 recruits aboard NTC Bainbridge. Even a dental technician training program fell under the realm of the Administrative Command.

Bainbridge would again be "mothballed," or in near-inactive status, in the mid-1950s. Finally new activities were brought to the base to breathe new life into Bainbridge, which brought a huge sigh of relief to local citizenry, as Bainbridge had been the area's major civilian employer during periods of activity.

New activities from the Bureau of Naval Personnel, the only WAVE-recruit training command in the United States (1951); the Enlisted Personnel Distribution Office, Continental United States (1958); and the Personnel Accounting Machine Installation, Continental United States (1959) kept Bainbridge active. In 1962, a nuclear-power school was added, and in 1963, the Naval Reserve Manpower Center was established at Bainbridge, as tenants of the base. Service School Command, the largest and oldest organization at Bainbridge after recruit training ended, was still training over 2,000 personnel in the 1970s in radioman A and B, fire-control technician A and C, yeoman A and C, and personnelman C-1 recruiter schools. Training was offered to learn skills as a postal clerk, teleman, hospital corpsman, or quartermaster. In 1953, the School of Recruit Procurement has been transferred from Norfolk, Virginia, and in 1959, a Naval Security Group Detachment opened.

The base was also alive with the community activities one might expect from the Navy Wives Club, including chapel, kindergarten, and Easter sunrise services. There were concerts and dances, performances by the Baltimore Symphony Orchestra, a theater group, Boy Scouts, Cub Scouts, Little League, and tours of the base for local schoolchildren. Camp Concern came to the base during the Nixon era, bringing Baltimore's inner-city children to the pastoral base for fun and activities.

Bainbridge appeared to once again be an active and bustling military installation in the early 1960s, but before the decade ended, the signs would change and point to a return to inactivity once again. The schools at Bainbridge started closing one by one, their former classrooms gradually drifting into dusty empty rooms. In May 1972, the last WAVE Company graduated, then the Nuclear Power School—the last school remaining on the base—closed. The death knell tolled mournfully in 1976, when after the closure of the schools and camps, the base itself was finally closed.

The once-proud base for training sailors was considered for myriad uses by planners and various elected officials, all while the federal Job Corps program, under authority of the Department of Labor, utilized the property and buildings for teaching mostly delinquent youth job skills. During this period, the Tome School buildings as well as some other navy-era buildings continued in use for education purposes, but this was also a period, according to contemporary newspaper articles, that saw wanton destruction and vandalism, riots, and arson fires on the base. The Job Corps program operated at Bainbridge for 11 years, and eventually the local Cecil Community College began a truck-driver training program, using the old roads of what was essentially an abandoned city.

Meanwhile, studies and theories were generated on how to best use the large swath of property, hopefully to the benefit of Cecil County and the small communities that had suffered terribly upon the closing of the base. Ideas were put forth for a federal prison facility, a NASCAR track and support facilities, Hollywood East, a rubble quarry and landfill, a nuclear-power plant, even a theme park, while the base withered away and nature swiftly reclaimed the property.

After fits and starts and a lengthy clean-up process in which buildings containing asbestos and lead paint were bulldozed and buried in a deep ravine that became a monitored hillside along Jacob Tome Highway, another change was on its way to Bainbridge. In 1997, through the efforts of Delegate David Rudolph, a group of Port Deposit residents, all members of Port Deposit Heritage Corporation, formed the Tome School Clean-Up Volunteers. Every Saturday, from May through October, the volunteers gathered on base to hack away at weeds and overgrowth and reclaim the Tome School—later NAPS—area of the base.

Finally, through special legislation in the Maryland General Assembly, the Bainbridge Development Corporation, composed of local volunteers, was created to take on the task of redeveloping the property. The town of Port Deposit, in 1999, annexed the property into its town limits, including the two National Historic Districts of Tome School for Boys and Snow Hill, the site of a pre–Civil War, free black community on the outskirts of the base.

Valentine's Day, February 14, 2000, a crowd gathered under a tent in the parking lot at the main gate to witness the final formal turnover of Bainbridge from the federal government to the State of Maryland and the Bainbridge Development Corporation. Even without a drill team or a flag pole with which to hold a flag-lowering ceremony, the event was moving, and to those who had attended both the 1976 closing ceremony and this the turnover ceremony 24 years later, the 2000 event was more emotionally charged and auspicious. The turnover ceremony featured the ceremonial passing of the last Bainbridge flag, which is now on permanent display at the Paw Paw Museum in Port Deposit, the signing of a ceremonial deed, and the final playing of "Anchors Aweigh."

Since February 14, 2000, the Bainbridge Development Corporation has met with numerous entities with business plans and redevelopment concepts for the old base. They have set aside land for a Bainbridge Navy Museum, while the Bainbridge Historical Association continues to gather and archive memorabilia, ephemera, documentation, and relics, displaying only a small portion of their collection in rented space along Port Deposit's waterfront. Paul Risk Associates, based in Quarryville, Pennsylvania, and Port Deposit, Maryland, have taken on the daunting task of stabilizing the Tome School for Boys buildings, all of which have been condemned and have suffered needlessly from vandalism, fire, water damage, and neglect. The company has created a unique plan for adaptive reuse of the historic structures, all built of Port Deposit granite, into a continuous-care facility.

Although there is little left to identify Bainbridge to visitors today as viewed through the rusting chain-link fence, save crumbling foundations, old pothole-ridden roads, and the occasional sign or glimpse of a failing structure, these last vestiges will soon, too, be gone. In their place, through the efforts of Bainbridge Development Corporation and their development partners, will be a new and vibrant community. Bainbridge and its great service to this country, however, will be recalled through signage, a navy museum on the property, the adaptive reuse of the Tome area, and the men and women who continue to serve its memory.

One

Before and During the Wartime Building Boom

Prior to 1941–1942, the bluff above the tiny town of Port Deposit in Cecil County, Maryland, was dotted with small farms, businesses, and homes, even a few failed towns—Heckarttown, Hawkinsville, Gurleytown, and Snow Hill, a free black community prior to 1841. Some 100 acres of the bucolic landscape changed forever upon the death of Cecil County's first millionaire, Jacob Tome, in 1898. He left the free private school he had founded in 1894, the Jacob Tome Institute, and its board of trustees the equivalent of $3 million in his will. The school board opted to build a private boarding school for boys on the bluff above town, naming it Tome School for Boys.

The school was successful but fell on hard times following the Great Depression, and it was eventually put on the market. Pres. Franklin D. Roosevelt was advised of the availability and signed an executive order purchasing the campus and acquiring some 71 surrounding properties to create a 1,132-acre military base, which eventually went to the U.S. Navy for training and operational purposes. The Beaux-Arts-designed school buildings would become the Naval Academy Preparatory School, or NAPS, and the rest of the property would be hastily converted from pastures and farms to drill fields and barracks during a crash wartime building boom.

The time frame was so rapid, in fact, that it necessitated sending airplanes over Southern states to drop thousands of leaflets recruiting workers to build the base or work in factories in Cecil County. The town of Port Deposit was also changed forever, as massive homes were converted to boarding houses for construction workers, who often slept in shifts, renting beds for a period of hours.

JACOB TOME, 1810–1898. Cecil County's first millionaire and Port Deposit's greatest philanthropist, he founded the Jacob Tome Institute for the town's children and left a fortune for the school in his will. The Tome School for Boys campus, built in 1900 to 1905 in his name and using this endowment, became the central purchase that would make up the Bainbridge Naval Training Center some 40 years later. (Courtesy of Paw Paw Museum.)

Tome School and Mansion House. Port Deposit. Md.   3

WASHINGTON HALL, 1894. Known originally as Building No. 1, this was the first structure of the Jacob Tome Institute on Port Deposit's Main Street, which opened in 1894 as a free school for Port Deposit children. The building was later razed after the school was removed to North East, Maryland, and only the front arch remains. The Tome mansion, in the background, was torn down in 1948. (Courtesy of Paw Paw Museum.)

MEMORIAL HALL, BUILT 1900–1901. The centerpiece of the Tome School for Boys campus was the classroom building, which housed administrative offices, the library, laboratories, and auditorium. Built of dressed Port Deposit granite and dedicated to founder Jacob Tome, it was designed by New York architects Boring and Tilton after they completed the main building of the Ellis Island Immigrant Station. (Courtesy of Paw Paw Museum.)

THE ITALIAN GARDENS, C. 1907. No expense was spared to create a lush campus at Tome School for Boys under the eye of supervisor Frederick Law Olmsted, designer of New York's Central Park. He chose Charles Wilson Leavitt to design the gardens as a beautiful venue for study, reflection, and the occasional outdoor class, tea, or social event directly in front of the headmaster's house, in the background. (Tome School Prospectus, 1919–1920.)

TOME SCHOOL FOR BOYS CAMPUS, C. 1907. This image from a Tome School prospectus of 1919 gives a bird's-eye view of the campus showing the Italian Gardens and buildings radiating from the gardens. Each structure was made of dressed Port Deposit granite. Architects Boring and Tilton were hired after winning a competition held by the trustees for overall campus and building design. The campus included three dedicated boarding houses—Jackson, Harrison, and Madison;

a gymnasium called Monroe with an indoor swimming pool, batting cages, and theater area; a multipurpose building called the Van Buren House and the Tome or Chesapeake Inn or House, which housed younger boys, the dining hall, campus store, phaeton company, athletic store, and lounge and hotel facilities for guest speakers and visitors; and the centerpiece, Memorial Hall. (Tome School Prospectus, 1919–1920.)

JACKSON HOUSE, C. 1907. One of the first dormitories built on the Tome School for Boys Campus, this structure housed primarily senior boys, with each student having his own furnished room. Later navy personnel, including Bainbridge Historical Association president Mike Miklas, would be housed here. It was gutted by fire during the 11-year reign of Job Corps on the base and was subsequently condemned. (Tome School Prospectus, 1919–1920.)

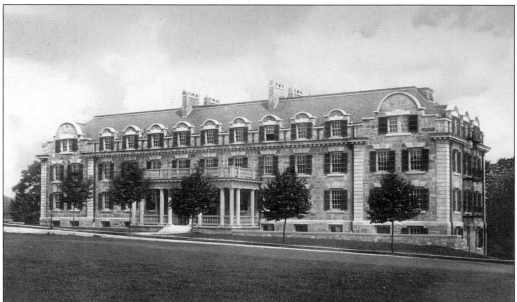

HARRISON HOUSE, BUILT C. 1905. The first dormitory seen on approach to the Tome campus, Harrison House was the last building constructed on campus. The architecture is slightly different than older structures, but it, too, is of dressed Port Deposit granite, which was laboriously hauled up the steep hillside by means of horse and wagon from the granite quarry on the extreme south side of the town. (Tome School Prospectus, 1919–1920.)

MADISON HOUSE, BUILT C. 1902. The smallest of the Tome dormitories, this structure was altered by the U.S. Navy. The side porches were removed to leave room for air-conditioning units and steel fire escapes. Also removed were the decorative front porches on the second story, although a ghostly outline of these porches remains on the condemned building. (Tome School Prospectus, 1919–1920.)

VAN BUREN HOUSE, BUILT C. 1901. Alternately called Tome or Chesapeake Inn or House, this granite structure was later covered in cedar shingles. It housed the youngest boys at Tome and later a 300-seat dining hall. The campus store and phaeton (early taxi) company were located inside, as was a lounge. Guest speakers, such as Franklin D. Roosevelt, and visiting families stayed here in rooms used strictly for visitors. (Tome School Prospectus, 1919–1920.)

MONROE HOUSE, BUILT C. 1901–1902. Also known as the Little Theater to Tome Boys, this building housed a moving-viewing area, massive fireplaces, and athletics facilities. The navy would utilize it for recreational purposes, too, as it had a lounge and club as well as the Monroe Room for receptions. A gymnasium to the rear of the facility once boasted outdoor batting cages as well. (*The Trail*, 1938.)

SWIMMING POOL, C. 1937. The indoor swimming pool at Tome was unique and was used for recreation and by a fine swim team, especially the team of 1938, from whence this photograph dates. The long, narrow pool room had a rounded ceiling with natural light from windows on either end and was completely tiled, including all walls, the ceiling, and hallways to the shower and locker areas. (*The Trail*, 1938.)

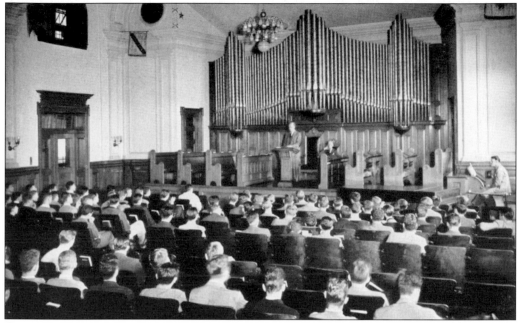

Chapel at Memorial Hall, Built c. 1901. Tome School boys attended chapel daily inside Memorial Hall's lovely auditorium, built in 1901. The beautiful pipe organ was removed by the navy, but three wooden pipes from it are retained by the Paw Paw Museum in Port Deposit. Here guest speakers addressed the student body throughout the year, which was capped off with commencement ceremonies. (*The Trail*, 1938.)

Classroom in Memorial Hall, 1938. Tome students, like the military students who would occupy classrooms later, learned at the feet of the best educators available. Students at Tome were in college-preparatory and business classes taught by graduates of Johns Hopkins, Yale, Dickinson, Princeton, MIT, and even the Naval Academy, an ironic precursor to the future use of the buildings. (*The Trail*, 1938.)

DINING HALL, BUILT C. 1907. Originally the boys at Tome dined in Monroe Hall, but this larger 300-seat dining hall was added to Van Buren House around 1907. The boys dined on white linen tablecloths, changed thrice daily, and white plates with a Tome-blue stripe and letter "T" adorning them, amid the splendor of a vaulted ceiling with gleaming wood floors and walls, as waiters in crisp white coats kept silver creamers and sugar bowls filled at each six-person table. (*The Trail*, 1938.)

DANCE COMMITTEE, 1938. There was a host of activities and organizations at Tome, including the Quill and Tome Literary Club, gun club, glee club, Pythians, Olympians, student council, band, a brief Ukelele Club, and the Dapper Dance Committee. Three annual dances were held, and in 1938, they were planned by the committee pictured here. Seen from left to right are Wesley Rae, Arnett Shaw, Frederic Saltmarsh, Bertram Davidson, and Preston Osteen. Dances were always white-tie affairs. (*The Trail*, 1938.)

DRAMA CLUB, C. 1915. The stage extended at Monroe Hall to accommodate footlights, and Tome School boys staged a number of productions, ranging from serious to tongue-in-cheek, classic to original, each year. As it was a school for boys, the performances were necessarily done in the Shakespearean style, much to the chagrin of some and ribald enjoyment of others in the student-body audience. (Courtesy of Paw Paw Museum.)

TOME BAND, C. 1915. Performances of the Tome Band were always popular at wildly well-attended sporting events, especially the annual interscholastic track meeting, which brought spectators on special trains from Baltimore. The song certain to get the crowd roaring was always the "Victory Song" with shouted lyrics of "Tome! Tome! To Victory! / We're going to win this game!" (Courtesy of Paw Paw Museum.)

STUDENTS AT MADISON HOUSE, C. 1915. Although each boy had his own room, these students hauled their brass beds to the porch of their dormitory, presumably on a fun lark. Pranks such as running shower curtains up the flagpole and cutting the lines or relocating beds to odd places on campus were frequent occurrences. (Courtesy of Paw Paw Museum.)

CAMPUS LIFE, C. 1915. Serious students during the day, the boarders and day boys who walked up the hill from town or arrived via train enjoyed a special camaraderie when time allowed in their busy daily schedules. Presumably in front of Madison Hall, these boys donned their pajamas and posed for a shutterbug for a rare candid image of student life. (Courtesy of Paw Paw Museum.)

TOME FOOTBALL, C. 1915. Donning leather helmets and a uniform emblazoned with a "T," the Tome boys fielded impressive football teams, even winning enough games in 1907 to have their winning scores carved into a slab of granite halfway down the trail to Port Deposit. That year, the Tome boys even managed to topple the Naval Academy's B team, a score that was also carved in stone. (Courtesy of Paw Paw Museum.)

TRACK MEET, C. 1915. Football drew a crowd but nothing like the ones at the annual interscholastic track meet on Tome's impressive cinder running track, reportedly the first of its kind in the state of Maryland. Concrete bleachers became crowded as spectators lined up for a glimpse of athletes setting new records in track and field and earning medals, gold pieces, and silver loving cups for doing so. (Courtesy of Paw Paw Museum.)

TOME BASEBALL, C. 1915. The boys on the diamond never managed to draw the large crowds football and track did, but they played impressively in their white wool uniforms with blue lettering. Occasionally one of the boys at the free-town school was so good at baseball that he would be recruited to trek up the hill and play ball with the "hill team" but returned to classes downtown thereafter. (Courtesy of Paw Paw Museum.)

BASEBALL GAME, C. 1915. A clever photographer managed a difficult action shot as Tome struck out another player on the diamond. Years later, this field would welcome the likes of Gene Tunney, Connie Mack, and Stan Musial, all of whom came to Bainbridge either as part of athletics programs on base, or, in Musial's case, as a recruit. (Courtesy of Paw Paw Museum.)

Tennis Courts, c. 1915. Tome always fielded excellent tennis teams, and the courts were popular for recreation as well. The courts remained during the navy years, with others added at different locations on base, and in the early 1970s, tennis was one of the most popular activities on the base, especially at the 70-year-old clay Tome courts where equipment was loaned out nearby. (Courtesy of Paw Paw Museum.)

Campus from the Courts, 1915. The tree-lined roads and sidewalks of Tome were best viewed from the tennis courts, as seen here with a view of the walk in front of Madison House. In fall, the trees were a riot of color, and in the summer, their huge canopies offered cooling shade for the buildings and acted as funnels for breezes across the campus quad. (Courtesy of Paw Paw Museum.)

THE TRAIL, C. 1915. One of the few extant indicators of the Tome campus is the foot of the Trail, which carried Tome day boys up the hill to school and boarders down to church services and sodas and sandwiches at "The Winnie," or Winchester's, on Main Street. Sailors also used the trail and in doing so passed Tome's Record Rock, near where these students were photographed. (Courtesy of Kevin Matthews.)

GRADUATION DAY, C. 1915. When this unidentified senior donned cap and gown, he never imagined his school would cease to exist in 25-odd years. In 1941, the last class graduated from Tome School for Boys, and at 11:00 a.m., March 28, 1942, the campus was sold for $964,494.80 to the federal government, courtesy of Pres. Franklin D. Roosevelt's executive order allocating the property to the navy. (Courtesy of Paw Paw Museum.)

Two

WELCOME ABOARD NTC BAINBRIDGE

Pres. Franklin D. Roosevelt did not take a great deal of time to decide on purchasing the campus of the struggling Tome School for Boys in 1941. As undersecretary of the U.S. Navy, he stayed at the Tome Inn and was a guest speaker in Memorial Hall for the assembled students. Roosevelt was therefore abundantly familiar with the beautiful campus overlooking the Susquehanna River.

Roosevelt acquired the then 335-acre campus for less than $1 million. Maryland senator Millard E. Tydings, ranking Democratic member of the Senate Naval Affairs Committee, announced in 1941 that the campus would be expanded to accommodate 20,000 naval recruits, with Tome serving as one of three major induction centers for naval recruits in the country. Through condemnation, another 1,000 acres was acquired, consisting of 71 privately owned homes and farms belonging to, among others, the Todd, Whitaker, Hagerty, Clapp, and Benson families.

The first crew of workmen from Charles H. Thompkins Company, of Washington, D.C., arrived in Port Deposit on May 7, 1942, to build NTC Bainbridge. Among them was V. T. "Ted" Middleton of Rising Sun, who said the workmen slept in rooms rented on a shift basis and that "the beds never had a chance to get cold." The first thing built at Bainbridge was a union office. "Then we built the thunder-boxes [outhouses]," Middleton recalled when interviewed in 1974 at the age of 71 years.

It took about two weeks to build a barracks at the four separate camps—each with its own drill hall and grinder—at a cost of about $1 million and six months of labor. Middleton, a foreman for the Thompkins Company, said it took 15,000 men and $50 million to transform the farmland into a naval base. Between May 19 and August 14, 1942, there were 506 temporary buildings erected, sans paved roads and an adequate water supply.

WELCOME-ABOARD SIGN, C. 1955. Though the letters were removed from this concrete sign after the base closed, the ghosts of the letters remained along Route 222. Thus, this simple concrete slab became one of the most photographed remnants of the former base a half century after it welcomed new recruits. (Courtesy of Mike Miklas.)

MAIN GATE, C. 1943. Drivers were cautioned to dim their lights as they approached the guard box at the gate on Bainbridge Road at the base. The main gate was off Route 222, through the sprawling parking area at the foot of Bainbridge Road. Ironically enough, years later, Route 222 would become known to many as Bainbridge Road. (Department of the Navy, Naval Historical Center.)

Training Center Emblem, c. 1955. Many a new recruit, or "boot," paused for a photograph at this sign, the emblem of the base, which became somewhat of a landmark to locals over the years. When the navy base was turned over the State of Maryland by the federal government in 2000, it was this image that was selected as the cover for the ceremonial program. (*The Compass*, 1955.)

Bainbridge Bus, c. 1955. The bus and driver wait as their passengers—new recruits—likely arrive courtesy the railroad at the Perryville Station nearby and enter the Processing or Receiving Unit, as another bus that had already discharged passengers heads back to the railroad station. (*The Compass*, 1955.)

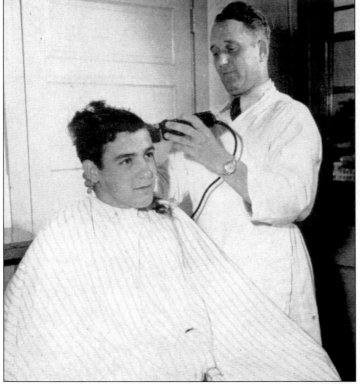

REAL CREW CUT, 1955. Mountains of paperwork were waded through before new recruits moved on to the next steps in their navy careers, including a stop at the barber for a real crew cut courtesy of a massive pair of clippers. According to one recruit at Bainbridge who arrived in 1943, "They made the loudest God-awful noise. . . . I thought they were taking my ears off, too!" (*The Compass*, 1955.)

HEARING CHECK, 1955. A full medical and dental examination was given to recruits, who were lined up in straight, close lines and marched past the awaiting doctor and technicians. The results of various tests were written down on clipboards, and brief notes were scrawled across the bare chests of the recruits before they went to the next testing station. (*The Compass*, 1955.)

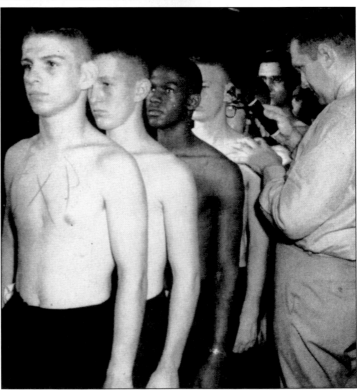

INOCULATION LINE, 1955. After recruits—three at a time on angled boards while standing (and usually looking away)—created their own tourniquet by squeezing their right arm with their left hand to allow technicians to draw blood, they were marched to the next station. Here they received shots in each arm, which often resulted in one or more of the men behind passing out. (*The Compass*, 1955.)

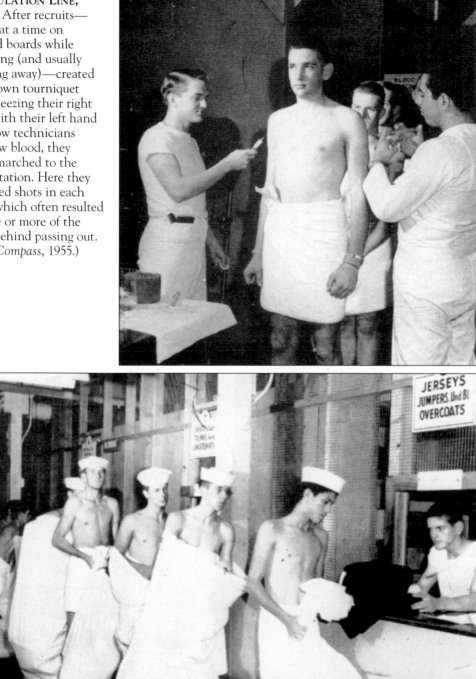

FILLING THE SEA BAG, 1955. After testing, screening, paperwork, and haircuts, recruits, with their towels snugly wrapped around their waists, were put into yet another line to visit the caged windows where they received their uniforms. They were measured from top to bottom and squared for the first time as they ran this gamut. The complete uniform was sized to allow recruits to gain a little muscle. (*The Compass*, 1955.)

STENCILING THE UNIFORM, 1955. The recruit was expected to maintain his uniform and gear at all times, and to help him do so more efficiently, every item each man received was laboriously stenciled with his name, an early task for each raw recruit. (*The Compass*, 1955.)

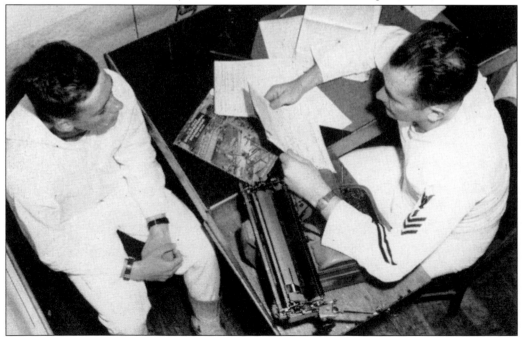

RECRUIT TESTING, 1955. A first-class personnelman is shown here conducting an individual interview with a new recruit. During the first day of in-processing, the classification process was begun through interviews and aptitude tests. Results were then analyzed to help determine to what navy job the recruit was best suited. (*The Compass*, 1955.)

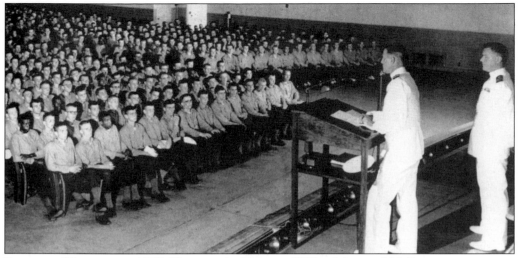

RECRUITS WELCOMED, 1955. Photographed here in 1955 in Memorial Hall, new recruits were welcomed aboard NTC Bainbridge. Most recruits, however, were seated in rows of chairs lined up in the drill halls of their various camps or regimental areas to receive a welcome from the commanding officer. (*The Compass,* 1955.)

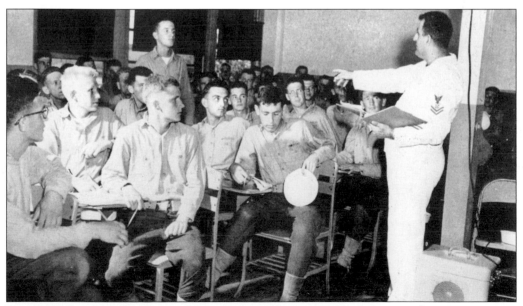

TRAINING CLASS, 1955. New recruits were greeted by instructors in a variety of training programs on the main campus of NTC Bainbridge. The recruits underwent weekly testing and near-constant drills on the material they were being taught. (*The Compass,* 1955.)

ANTI-AIRCRAFT GUN TRAINING, 1954. Recruits were given hands-on lessons in the handling, loading, and maintenance of numerous types of gunnery and ordnance, including this 20-mm anti-aircraft gun. (*The Compass*, 1955.)

RIFLE-RANGE TRAINING, 1955. Special precautions were always observed at the rifle range, where recruits fired .22-caliber rifles to gain practical knowledge and experience. One man would position himself and sight his target while sprawled across a mattress on the floor as his partner held a tray of ammunition at the ready for him to reload. (*The Compass*, 1955.)

RIFLE RANGE, 1943. A popular destination with the men, the rifle range was used for training purposes. At any given time, every single lane of the range would be filled with men, while at other times, as few as a dozen men honed their marksmanship skills. Occasionally an assembly of dozens of men might watch and learn from the efforts of one chosen marksman. (Library of Congress, Prints and Photographs Division, Gottscho-Schleisner Collection.)

NAVY KNOTS, C. 1944. Training continued in seasmanship, no matter what technical specialty the recruit drew. Scale models were used to teach fundamentals, along with instruction in wheel, magnetic compass, and engine-order telegraph. The men also received instruction in Marlinspike Seamanship, learning to tie knots, bend lines, and throw hitches. (U.S. Navy Photograph Postcard, courtesy of Kevin Matthews.)

THE COMMODORE, 1955. Because the station was named in honor of Commodore William Bainbridge, it was only fitting that the training vessel on base be dubbed the *Commodore*. However, most of the recruits referred to 401B, the recruit-training ship, as "The Never Sail." Here men put classroom knowledge to work and conducted general quarters drill. (*The Compass*, 1955.)

NAVY FIREFIGHTERS, 1955. Recruits learned the specialized skills necessary to fight fire aggressively and safely in unique situations presented aboard navy vessels, as well as on shore. The men were placed in small groups and tested in the field using a Billy Pump, all-purpose nozzles, and other equipment to check oil and gasoline fires in simulated shipboard compartments to mock aircraft and structural fires. (*The Compass*, 1955.)

NEW CHALLENGES, 1955. Once the recruits successfully learned their lessons in fighting fires, they moved on to new challenges. In the mid-1950s, these new challenges were classes for using equipment to quickly identify atomic, biological, and chemical attacks and to defend against them. (*The Compass*, 1955.)

CANNED SAFETY, 1955. These recruits were new to water-safety class, as they are still wearing what the navy referred to as "flotation devices" to help overcome their fear of water. Upon closer inspection, one notices that the flotation devices are actually cans looped about the waist of each recruit as they learn different water-safety techniques. (*The Compass*, 1955.)

ABANDON SHIP, 1954. The recruit who overcame his fear of water might have a new fear to overcome as part of the navy's water- and fitness-training regimen: the fear of jumping from a significant height into deep water. The sign above the jumping platform reads "Physical fitness thru abandon ship drills." (*The Compass*, 1955.)

STAMINA AND AGILITY TRAINING, 1954. Recruits at Bainbridge did not just have to learn water-safety skills; they also puzzled and sweated through obstacle and confidence courses, both of which required stamina and intense concentration to complete. In many instances, the men, broken into small groups, would be unable to complete the course without teamwork, another learning tool. (*The Compass*, 1955.)

NEARING THE FINISH LINE. After facing gauntlets of ropes to climb, ditches to swing across, tires to navigate, poles and stumps to cross, and monkey bars to navigate, the recruit still came up against an obstacle of thick rope rungs between two poles and cold murky water below before reaching the end of this confidence course. In 1999, remnants of a very similar course obstacle were found behind Memorial Hall during a Tome School Clean-Up Volunteers project. (*The Compass*, 1955.)

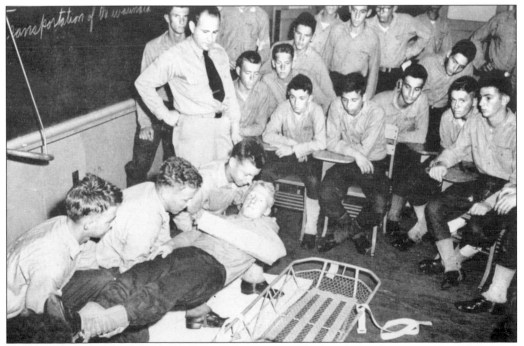

FIRST-AID TRAINING, 1955. Boots were being trained to enter battle situations, and first-aid training was a very important part of their lessons. The most modern practices of the day were employed first in classroom and then in mock emergency-drill situations at different locations for each regiment. (*The Compass*, 1955.)

GAS-MASK TRAINING, 1943. Unfortunately there was but one way to learn the importance of proper use of gas masks, and that was through a training exercise in the Bainbridge gas chamber. Here teary-eyed recruits exit the crudely built structure sitting on newly graded earth that was farmland two years prior, as, in the background, construction on the base continues. (Library of Congress, Prints and Photographs Division, Gottscho-Schleisner Collection.)

MILITARY DRILL, 1954. The techniques and training were many for military and physical drills—including position of ready; diagonal lunge; dress right, dress; Semaphore drill; present arms; and always, always rigid inspection. Drill played an important part in bringing the recruit's mind and body up to the high standard of mental and physical stamina demanded by naval duties, afloat or ashore. (*The Compass*, 1955.)

DRUM AND BUGLE CORPS, 1954. Special performances were held each week of Recruit Training as part of the graduation review, held on Saturdays on the Rodgers' Parade Field. The Drum and Bugle Corps provided special performances, as did the Recruit Band and both the WAVE and male drill teams. (*The Compass*, 1955.)

THE RECRUIT BAND, 1954. Prior to actual commencement, the command drill officer explained the review in an address to visiting relatives and friends. Then the review was conducted by recruits without assistance from battalion or company commanders. Here the recruit band passes in review on Rodgers' Parade Field, just in front of the Camp Rodgers Drill Hall. (*The Compass*, 1955.)

MASSING OF THE FLAGS, 1954. A solemn but beautiful sight was the massing of the colorful flags as part of the graduation review on the Rodgers' Parade Field. The black-and-white image cannot capture the pomp and ceremony of this commencement exercise, when the contrasts presented were of the white uniforms and whipping flags against the pristinely swept blacktop surface of the drill field. (*The Compass*, 1955.)

INSPECTING THE HONOR GUARD, 1954. Part of the pomp and circumstance of the graduation ceremonies was the inspection of the Honor Guard. The men maneuvered like clockwork with swift movements, and according to one observer, the crowd was so silent during this part of the ceremony that the click of shoes on the macadam could be heard distinctly. (*The Compass*, 1955.)

SAILORS ALL, 1943. It was just the beginning of their navy career as recruits or the end of their recruit training when they graduated that were moments of pride for the young men training at Bainbridge. These recruits, showing definitively the variety of sailors aboard Bainbridge, seem justifiably proud of the still under-construction base, their uniforms, and their training. (Library of Congress, Prints and Photographs Division, Gottscho-Schleisner Collection.)

COMPANY 4608, 1946. This folded photograph of Company 4608 was taken after graduation review. Note that the men are standing on hastily but sturdily built wood bleachers, and the grounds of the drill field are still unpaved and therefore were dusty in summer and muddy in winter and summer storms. Yet the men in this picture are justifiably proud of their hard work.

44

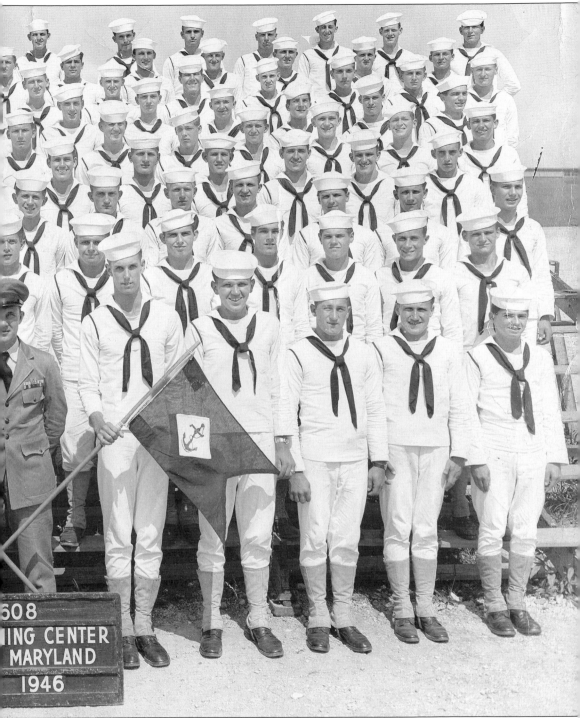

608
ING CENTER
MARYLAND
1946

This photograph was donated to the Bainbridge Historical Association by Orville March, PNCS, USN, Ret., who recorded the last name of nearly every man pictured on the reverse of the image. (Courtesy of Orville March, PNCS, USN, Ret.)

MARCH OF **WAVES, C. 1972.** WAVE Recruit Training Command came to Bainbridge in 1951 and stayed until 1972, when it was relocated to Orlando, Florida, after 21 years. In October 1951, exactly 104 WAVE recruits were welcomed aboard training at Bainbridge's new all-female boot-camp unit, later Recruit Training Command for Women. Here WAVE recruits are in graduation review in their massive drill in the 1st Regiment. (The *Mainsheet*, June 29, 1973.)

PROUD LADY **WAVES, C. 1970.** June 20, 1951, the first two WAVES reported aboard Bainbridge's Naval Hospital Command, Hospital Corpsman 3c Marion Walsh of New York and Hospitalman Fran Griffith of Portsmouth, Ohio, from the Philadelphia Naval Hospital. WAVES were a proud and striking addition to Bainbridge and carry on their tradition of service and pride today at reunions and events. (The 1970 Unofficial Guide to Bainbridge.)

THE FAMOUS SIGN, C. 1969. Every WAVE knows by rote the words of this famous sign, which new recruits passed under every two weeks on their way to processing. Here some new recruits in the 1960s gather before passing through those historic portals to become part of yet another company of WAVES. "This moment, it is said, brings a lump to the girls' throats now and years later when they remember the moment," reads the 1970 Unofficial Guide to Bainbridge. (The 1970 Unofficial Guide to Bainbridge.)

SYMBOL OF THE COMMAND. This diamond-shaped symbol is still a thing of pride to WAVES. In August 1962, RTC(W) was made a separate command with a commanding officer. Staffed by 7 WAVE officers and 55 enlisted women, the command graduated about 2,400 recruits yearly, with reviews held every other week on Friday mornings. Recruit WAVES received 10 weeks of intensive basic training but still found a little time for record hops, picnics, songfests, movies, and swim meets. (The 1970 Unofficial Guide to Bainbridge.)

HUNTER HALL, 1971. Seen through the saluting arm of a WAVE, Hunter Hall was dedicated and occupied as the WAVE-recruit barracks on February 24, 1967. The H-shaped structure afforded rooms shared by four recruits each and equipped with single beds, wardrobes, study desks, and lamps. Each of the six wings had its own recruit lounge, laundry, ironing and storage area, heads, and showers. Designed to house 452 recruits, the building was named as a tribute to Hunter College, where more than 86,000 enlisted women trained for naval service during World War II. (The 1970 Unofficial Guide to Bainbridge.)

ENDS OF THE EARTH. These two WAVES pinpoint their destination for their first duty stations as they prepare to leave Bainbridge after graduation. Bainbridge WAVES elected one of several areas of specialization—clerical and administrative ratings such as yeoman, machine accountant, or radioman; hospital and dental corps; or aviation and technical ratings to become photographers, aerographers, air control men, and electronics technicians. (The 1970 Unofficial Guide to Bainbridge.)

Three

NAVY LIFE AT NTC BAINBRIDGE

USNTC Bainbridge was commissioned October 1, 1942, and the 506 navy buildings constructed thereon were designed to serve for one decade, though they continued in use for 31 years. Bainbridge was named by Pres. Franklin D. Roosevelt in honor of the naval hero Commodore William Bainbridge, commander of the *Constitution*, a navy war frigate immortalized in the poem "Old Ironsides."

At Bainbridge, recruits and personnel would find a family-service center, providing welcome-aboard kits, maps, housing information, hospitality kits, and referrals, and a reference library in the Community Center Building. Building 720 housed an educational-services office. The dental department was in Building 708; there was the Center Hospital; and the chaplain's office was staffed with two Catholic and three Protestant chaplains. Aside from the specialized schools and commands, one could find entertainments for free time, too.

Bainbridge offered tennis courts, a nine-hole golf course with a water hazard and towering trees, swimming pools (both indoors and outdoors), an automobile hobby shop, a ceramic hobby shop near the Center Bank, a carpenter shop, riding stables, a pistol and rifle range, a bowling alley, a boat dock, a theater, and a library complete a three-channel stereo sound system in the early 1970s. The base wouldn't be complete, however, without the Navy Exchange in a building that also featured beauty shops, laundry, cobble pick-up, a barbershop, and the popular Navy Exchange Cafeteria. The commissary store, manned by civilians in 1972, was the supermarket for the 4,000 families then stationed there.

Rounding out the offerings were the "O" Club Bar, lounge, game room, Monroe Room, CPO Mess, EM and PO and Acey Ducey Club, CPO Bar, and Fiddler's Green EM Club.

First Recruit, 1942. Damon Sutton, a 19-year-old from Pittsburgh, was the first recruit aboard NTC Bainbridge when it was commissioned October 1, 1942. He was the first of thousands but the only one to receive such an auspicious welcome as pictured in a final edition of the *Mainsheet* in 1973. The fuzzy historic photograph from 1942 shows Capt. C. F. Russell, first commander at Bainbridge, welcoming Sutton. (The *Mainsheet*, 1973.)

Building 720. According to the 1970 Unofficial Guide to Bainbridge, a lot of paper was pushed in this building, Center Headquarters, which was near the center of the base. The guide notes, "Personnel paperwork piles prove personnelmen patient, perseverant." Officers and enlisted personnel reporting aboard for duty or instruction received check in/out cards here, and changes in rate, ability, or status were processed here. (The 1970 Unofficial Guide to Bainbridge.)

BIRD'S-EYE VIEW, 1970. Although not the most detailed of photographs, this bird's-eye view is one of the few that shows the base nearly in its entirety, save for the boat docks along the Susquehanna River and the Tome Area, which just couldn't fit in the frame. This photograph was taken of Bainbridge from 10,000 feet. The large rectangular open areas are the drill fields, and at the lower right is the Manor Heights housing area. (Courtesy of Mike Miklas.)

SAILOR'S WEDDING. Many a navy family lived in the Manor Heights area of Bainbridge. This wedding photograph is of sailor Ed Ellison with his new bride, the former Elmina Martin, and her parents. When his navy career ended, Ed became an active member of Bainbridge reunions and in the preservation of both Bainbridge and local Cecil County history. (Courtesy of Ed Ellison.)

DENTAL DEPARTMENT, C. 1967. Building 708 on Bainbridge Road housed the dental department, offering services to some 6,000 active duty and retired personnel by 1970. There were specialty sections for operative dentistry, prosthodontics, periodontics, endodontics, and exodontia, and X-rays and examinations were offered. Ten to 12 dental officers, a hygienist, a receptionist, a chief, and 16 dental technicians made emergency treatment available 24 hours a day. (The 1970 Unofficial Guide to Bainbridge.)

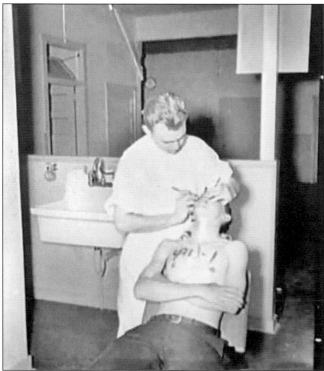

DENTAL EXAM, 1943. All recruits to Bainbridge were given a complete dental exam and eventually were able to avail themselves of the extensive line of dental services and procedures offered at the Bainbridge Dental Department. Many of the recruits who opened wide for the exam ended up taking specialized training as dental technicians at Bainbridge. (Library of Congress, Prints and Photographs Division, Gottscho-Schleisner Collection.)

ST. PAUL'S CHAPEL, 1943. The center chapel was erected in the Prairie School of design and could seat 40 people. By the 1970s, the chaplain's office was staffed with two Catholic and three Protestant chaplains, and five services and Mass were held every Sunday. There were also Latter-Day Saint, Church of Christ, Jewish, and Christian Science services held in Building 617 weekly. Chaplain staff was also in charge of the nursery and base kindergarten. Over the years, St. Paul's Chapel was the scene of intimate weddings and touching baptisms of children as well as holiday services. This sailor, heading for services in 1943, was one of many who availed themselves of the small but elegant building and the comfort offered therein. "I admit, I cried like a baby when they tore that building down, it was just so beautiful," said Mike Miklas, president of NTC Bainbridge Historical Association in 2006. (Department of the Navy, Naval Historical Center.)

BUILDING 601, C. 1968. The Enlisted Personnel Distribution Office, Continental United States (EPDOCONUS) was established and commissioned at Bainbridge in January 1960. Housed in Building 601, the personnel here handled all naval personnel throughout the continental United States, for some 60,000 billets. Working with the data-processing abilities of Personnel Accounting Machine Installation, Continental United States, EPDOCONUS retained 13 officers, 51 enlisted personnel, and 21 civilians for their use. (The 1970 Unofficial Guide to Bainbridge.)

MANPOWER IN READINESS, c. 1969. Naval Reserve Manpower Center (NRMC) was established in 1963 to provide rapid personnel mobilization and data in a crisis situation. Service and health records were maintained and correspondence processed, and an average of 13,000 pieces of mail were handled each day. Some 315 men and women worked here to keep things moving, maintaining 500,000 service records, 300,000 health records, and 225,000 officer classifications in one building. (The 1970 Unofficial Guide to Bainbridge.)

NUCLEAR POWER SCHOOL, C. 1969. On July 1, 1962, the Nuclear Power School (NUPS) was commissioned at Bainbridge out of New London, Connecticut, when the expanding nuclear-submarine program overtaxed the New London's facilities. NUPS was staffed by 56 instructors and 30 personnel and included courses in complex mathematics, classical physics, reactor principles and technology, nuclear physics, thermodynamics, and chemistry. (The 1970 Unofficial Guide to Bainbridge.)

POWER-OF-KNOWLEDGE SLOGAN, C. 1968. Every three months, a group of 300 carefully screened enlistees and 50 officer students were admitted to the Nuclear Power School, where they would pass under the quote above the doors reading, "Man's way through life is sustained by the power of his knowledge." Upon completion of the course, NUPS students were sent to prototype reactors for six months of additional training and then on to the nuclear fleet. (The 1970 Unofficial Guide to Bainbridge.)

EXPERIENCED INSTRUCTORS, C. 1969. The Nuclear Power School offered individual instruction with teachers on duty each evening and during working hours to help students with difficult problems. Among the men at NUPS in 1970 were Ens. Robert Kessler, Annapolis Class of 1965, pictured here with his instructor Lt. F. E. Naef, a veteran of three Polaris submarine patrols on the USS *Theodore Roosevelt*. (The 1970 Unofficial Guide to Bainbridge.)

MACHINE POWER, C. 1969. The Personnel Accounting Machine Installation, Continental United States, was established at Bainbridge in 1959. It was one of three installations maintaining naval personnel records in a data-processing center using a disk-oriented IBM 360/40 system, a tape-oriented IBM 1460 system, and a tape-oriented IBM 1401 system. Keypunch operators transferred coded data to individual IBM cards, which were fed at 1,000 to 2,000 cards per minute. (The 1970 Unofficial Guide to Bainbridge.)

RADIOMAN SCHOOL, c. 1969. Bainbridge hosted "A" and "B" Schools for radioman training, a crucial training program under the Service School Command. Communications was often referred to as the backbone of the U.S. Navy. The training offered was lengthy, difficult, and technical at the largest of the service schools—the A School—which had about 1,000 students. The B School was an advanced technical 36-week course. (The 1970 Unofficial Guide to Bainbridge.)

YEOMAN SCHOOL, c. 1968. The Service School Command's yeoman school at Bainbridge was divided into two classes, "A" and "C." Class A prepared sailors and WAVES for general administrative and clerical duties. The Class C school prepared advanced personnel for future secretarial duties with specialized training in shorthand and administrative functions. (The 1970 Unofficial Guide to Bainbridge.)

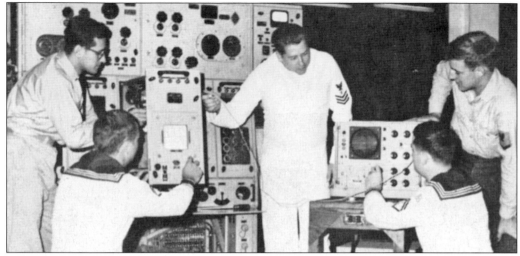

FIRE-CONTROL-TECHNICIAN SCHOOL. The Service School Command offered fire-technician students "A" and "C" Schools. The Class A students were trained in principles of electronic control of fire with mathematics, basic electronics, and computer systems. The Class C training was conducted in the majority of gunfire control systems for U.S. and Allied students—usually about 50 students from countries such as Greece, Japan, South America, and Portugal. (The 1970 Unofficial Guide to Bainbridge.)

RECRUITER SCHOOL, C. 1969. To fulfill the navy's manpower requirements with qualified personnel is the job of navy recruiters, and to assist them, the navy created the position of personnelman "C-1," basically a recruiter school at Bainbridge. Top petty officers were trained at the school in the "art of enlisting and re-enlisting" the best for the navy. A handcrafted stand-alone sign is part of the public-relations campaign planned by these five recruiters. (The 1970 Unofficial Guide to Bainbridge.)

PRIDE OF THE CENTER, C. 1968. The men of the Radioman "A" drill team were ambassadors of the navy from Bainbridge, marching in local parades and appearing at community events throughout Cecil and Harford Counties. They trained long hours each week on their own time. In 1968, they were called upon to render first aid at a train wreck and, for that service, were awarded a unit citation. Their leader was awarded a Legion of Merit Medal. (The 1970 Unofficial Guide to Bainbridge.)

TOME AREA, 1969. Midshipmen candidates of Naval Academy Preparatory School (NAPS) underwent nine months of instruction but also enjoyed a full program of athletics and extracurricular activities. They could participate in football, cross-country, basketball, wrestling, swimming, lacrosse, tennis, and track teams. Twice each day, the NAPS student battalion formed for muster and inspection in front of Memorial Hall. (The 1970 Unofficial Guide to Bainbridge.)

GRADUATION, C. 1969. The Naval Academy Preparatory School, on the old Tome campus, provided intensive instruction and guidance to prepare enlisted members of the U.S. Navy and U.S. Marine Corps for the naval academy. Students of NAPS send their caps soaring in the traditional salute at commencement exercises held each May in the formal Italian Gardens of the prep school area. (The 1970 Unofficial Guide to Bainbridge.)

MEMORIAL HALL LINE-UP, C. 1965. The line of midshipmen in the foreground gives a sense of scale and highlights the sheer magnitude of Memorial Hall, the main building of the Tome area that served as the Naval Academy Preparatory School during the navy years. (*The Compass*, 1955.)

SCULLERY DETAIL, C. 1954. The joy of pots and pans was experienced by all recruits. This was no small feat when one considers that each mess hall had eight chow lines each with their own serving dishes and utensils. A typical dinner in the 1940s included vegetable soup, Swiss steak with gravy, mashed potatoes, spinach, hard-boiled eggs, celery and cabbage salad, raisin and apple pie, bread and butter, coffee, milk, and pudding. (*The Compass*, 1955.)

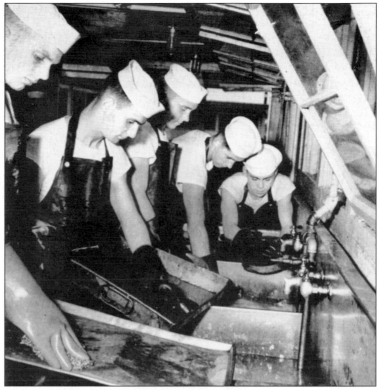

MESSENGER DETAIL, EARLY 1950s. Bainbridge was a large base with rolling topography, which seemed more like a series of stiff hills when hiking. This messenger drew the task of delivering schedules to all regimental areas, a chore made somewhat easier by his single-speed bike with large rubber tires. It must have been difficult to keep his uniform spotless while riding through some of the rougher streets during the rain. (*The Compass*, 1955.)

GROUNDS DETAIL, 1943. This work detail of enlisted men is well prepared for the daunting task of keeping the 1,132 acres of NTC Bainbridge lush, green, and pristine as part of a landscaping assignment. All of the recruits were expected to maintain the base, and whether the task was lawn care or swabbing the deck, guarding clotheslines or manicuring flower beds with scissors, the work was done with navy pride. (Department of the Navy, Naval Historical Center.)

SMALL BOAT TRAINING, 1943. After a hike down the steep bluff, these sailors crossed Port Deposit's Main Street to get to the navy boat docks and whale boats, where they would be trained in maneuvers on the swift-moving Susquehanna River. Images of the extensive boat docks the navy built along Port Deposit's waterfront are rare, and this image, taken in 1943, of small-boat training under oars is one of the few that survive. (Department of the Navy, Naval Historical Center.)

MAIL CALL, C. 1955. Perhaps the most welcoming sound at any military installation has always been the two words "mail call." With a stack of envelopes in hand, some with sweet-smelling perfume and others with photographs tucked inside, one man would call out names and pass out the cherished missives, which were read line for line, over and over again, by the recruits hungry for news from back home. (*The Compass*, 1955.)

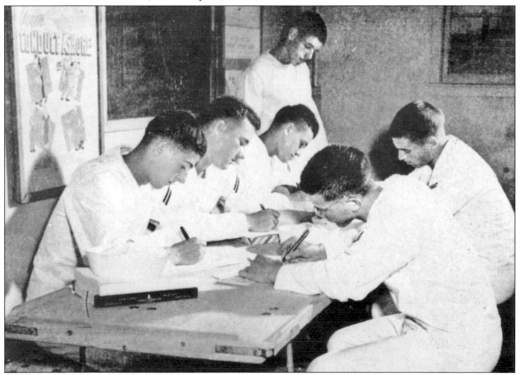

LETTERS HOME, C. 1955. Although their days were quite busy, the recruits always took time to pen a letter home to tell of life in the navy. Often they'd simply scratch a few lines on a navy postcard depicting various scenes of military life, and sometimes they sent long missives, occasionally accompanied by some heartfelt memento, such as a Bainbridge pillowcase, souvenir booklet, or other trinket. (*The Compass*, 1955.)

FIGHTING MEN, 1943. Looking at the disparity of size between these three enlisted men, it seems almost a miracle that the ship's store could find clothes to fit each of them. Tallest to shortest, they each appear to be fresh-faced lads better suited to the school room than to entering combat in World War II after only a few short weeks of training at Bainbridge. The first recruit to arrive at Bainbridge was 19 years old, and it certainly was not uncommon for men of a younger age to pass through the gates of NTC Bainbridge. Nonetheless, these men, young and old, novice or seasoned, forged bonds tested in the fire of war and formed a brotherhood born of military service that will never be torn apart. (Department of the Navy, Naval Historical Center.)

Four

BARRACKS LIFE AT BAINBRIDGE

A large percentage of a recruit's time was spent in and around his barracks learning how to live in peace in fairly cramped quarters. Of course, cleanliness proved to be next to godliness, but the men were also trained to exhibit good manners and personal conduct and to be considerate of others.

The men were always in a state of readiness with daily inspections of the barracks and of recruits, not just for proper cleanliness but also for proper storage in shipboard-type lockers or in a sea bag. Woe unto the man, or WAVE, who was found untidy or whose gear was unkempt, for they might be denied the opportunity to attend a record hop, the movies, an outing to the bowling alley, or one of the clubs on base. Worse yet, they might be assigned the dreaded detail of guarding the clotheslines for countless hours of mind-numbing boredom amidst clouds of white clothes snapping in the wind.

"There were quite a lot of dances at Bainbridge I remember, and I heard a lot of really great music performed at Bainbridge at the amphitheater," recalled Mike Miklas, who lived at Manor Heights but as a bachelor bunked at Jackson House at NAPS. "I can still remember like it was yesterday playing golf on that nine-hole course. It was always kept in tip-top shape and was a beautiful course to play. I played there even after I was out of the Navy, it was that nice of a course."

LAUNDRY DETAIL, 1955. Stenciled shirts on the backs of these men reveal the names Jeffers and Rulse as they stand at the wooden wash basins, where buckets of warm, soapy water, a bar of strong soap, and a tap of clean, cold water were available for the men to wash their clothing daily by the old "knuckle-busting" method. (*The Compass*, 1955.)

LAUNDRY DAY, 1943. Since the method of hand washing worked so well in 1943, not much changed at Bainbridge; even the same wooden washing areas were used for well over a decade. Perhaps that is why a dry cleaner, which opened just outside the main gate, and laundries in the area did so well during the navy days. (Department of the Navy, Naval Historical Center.)

GUARDING THE LINE, 1955. Once the clothes were bright white and clean, they were hung on the lines to dry just outside the barracks. Those billowing clouds of whites just might prove too much of a temptation, apparently, even though each was stenciled with someone's name. Therefore, alert sentries were assigned the duty of guarding the clotheslines, a theme that seems to persist in letters written home from the 1940s through the 1970s. (*The Compass*, 1955.)

SHIP SHAPE, C. 1954. With hats in hand, uniforms crisp, and bunks arranged properly, these recruits stand at attention as the battalion commander conducts a daily personnel inspection. These men may be standing with hat in hand for quite some time, as the commander seems to be in no particular hurry to get through the line as he minutely inspects the lining of one of the recruit's hats. (*The Compass*, 1955.)

LOCKER INSPECTION, C. 1952. Standing at stiff attention and looking straight ahead, this recruit appears to be ready and prepared for his locker inspection. His gear is tucked neatly away according to the regulations he has learned by rote, and his uniform appears to be freshly laundered and in good order. He'll likely receive no dressing down and be able to enjoy a sigh of relief and some free time. (*The Compass*, 1955.)

COMPANY COMMANDER, C. 1955. The inspections and need for perfect order and tidiness might prove exhausting and nerve-wracking to the recruits, but every so often the company commander would let down his guard, as it were, if he found no fault with the inspection. Though this photograph was staged for yearbook filler, there are many stories of commanders and recruits who formed lasting bonds and friendships. (*The Compass*, 1955.)

TENNIS COURTS, 1970. Tennis was very popular at Bainbridge in the late 1960s and early 1970s. Any time of day would find someone enjoying one of the eight courts available—four of which were championship-quality clay courts. In 1969, the regional and district navy competitions were held at Bainbridge, which boasted the best courts in the Fifth Naval District. (The 1970 Unofficial Guide to Bainbridge.)

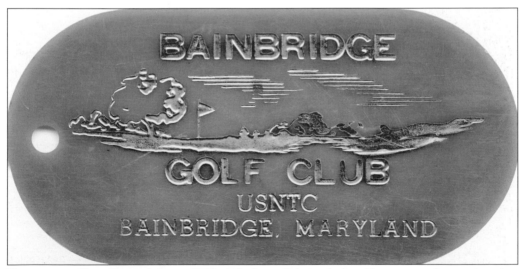

BAINBRIDGE GOLF COURSE, LATE 1960s. The beautiful nine-hole golf course was the continuation of the old Tome School for Boys golf course. The course hosted district, regional, and all-navy competitions for several years in the 1960s but was most often home to friendly and sometimes not-so-friendly competition amongst the men. This rare plastic bag tag was a cherished memento of one such golfer. (Courtesy of Mike Miklas.)

GOLFING TROPHY, LATE 1960s. The links were always busy at the Bainbridge Golf Course, and lucky was the man or woman who could book one of the two golf carts. The course being only nine holes, it could be walked fairly easily. In this rare photograph, Comdr. Skip White awards one of seven trophies and one grand prize golf bag to a lucky golfer, whose name has been lost to history, during the Fifth Naval District Tournament. (Courtesy of Mike Miklas.)

HOLE IN ONE, MID-1960s. Although the golf course featured but nine holes, it was popular, especially with the layout that utilized old trees and rolling terrain to create challenges. Mike Miklas, who used to play the links there, remembered that he had both his best and worst games on that course. This was a popular photograph used to advertise the links throughout the base. (The 1970 Unofficial Guide to Bainbridge.)

WAVES in the Pool, 1960s. Year-round swimming was available at Bainbridge's indoor and outdoor swimming pools, with hours varying upon the season. Noontime swimming for physical fitness was popular among NTC personnel. Outdoor pools were near the gas station and the officer's club and indoors at Buildings 401 and 101, and the oldest indoor pool was in the Tome Area at the O Club. Others were located in drill halls. Here a group of WAVES takes to the water in the indoor pool. (The 1970 Unofficial Guide to Bainbridge.)

Automobile Hobby Shop, 1960s. Seemingly always in use by young men and women polishing or repairing their automobiles, this building was a popular destination for many. Naval personnel had use of all tools needed to maintain their cars free of charge. An arc-welding outfit and acetelyne-welding-and-cutting facilities were on site as well as valve-grinding machines, tire changers, grease guns, lube pits, and washing stalls. (The 1970 Unofficial Guide to Bainbridge.)

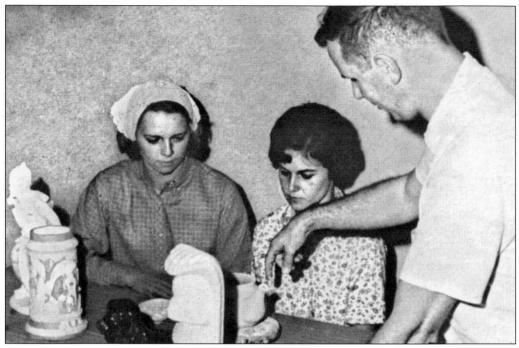

CERAMIC HOBBY SHOP. Building 508, adjacent to the Center Bank, housed this shop, which offered a selection of unbaked clay items (green ware), assorted paints, molds, wet clay (slip), and six kilns for firing. Weekly classes were held over the winter months for those interested in learning about ceramics. The Center Library also offered a number of books on ceramics, one of which was written by Port Deposit artist Paul Honore and is now part of the collection at the Paw Paw Museum in Port Deposit. (The 1970 Unofficial Guide to Bainbridge.)

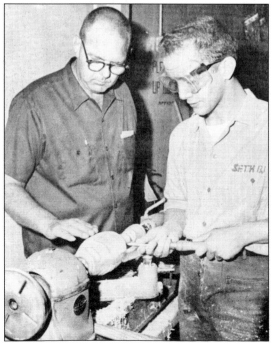

CARPENTER SHOP, C. 1969. Large and small tools were available for personnel interested in constructing such wood products as model ships, bookcases, shelves, and other items for their personal use or to give as gifts. The shop carried black walnut fir, Philippine mahogany, cherry, ponderosa pine, and interior plywood for use by the carpenters, as well as lathes and other equipment for making custom items, many of which are now treasured mementos of Bainbridge's carpenter shop in local collections. (The 1970 Unofficial Guide to Bainbridge.)

RIDING STABLES, C. 1969. One of the oft-discussed unique topics about Bainbridge was the riding stable, which was added in the 1960s as part of the Special Services Division and was a fitting addition to a base in horse country. The stable had 20 horses, a barn, and riding areas, along with associated tack and hardware. Riding instruction was offered to all naval personnel and their dependants, a popular feature with children on base, who could also work at the stables. (The 1970 Unofficial Guide to Bainbridge.)

DRILL HALLS, C. 1969. Although Bainbridge boasted four massive drill halls, by 1970, Drill Hall 401 was used primarily for recreation and Drill Hall 101 was for WAVES training. The other two halls were used for storage. At 401, basketball, boxing, swimming, and volleyball were offered, as well as general recreation during snowed-in winter months. Boy Scouts visited 401 during the summer on their way to the National Jamboree, and practice for the drum and bugle corps and bands was held therein. By the late 1960s, three squash courts and a sauna bath had been added to Building 401. (The 1970 Unofficial Guide to Bainbridge.)

BAINBRIDGE CHOIR, C. 1955. It might be expected that the base would offer a drum and bugle corps and regimental bands, but a choir might not be as expected. This choir from 1955 performed during services at St. Paul's Chapel, which must have proved a musical challenge for the choir director, as men and voices changed on base with such regularity. (*The Compass*, 1955.)

MUSIC FOR OFF-DUTY TIME, C. 1955. Bainbridge had a staff of CPOs, civilian librarians, and recreation directors who toiled to offer amusement and entertainment to recruits during off-duty hours. A recreation building in each regimental area offered everything from bowling to Ping-pong, billiards to a pool, board games to television, radio to records, as well as a library, magazines, reading room, and more. Men could find their own entertainment through the talents of a fellow recruit or visit the Navy Exchange, snack bar, or soda fountain as well. (*The Compass*, 1955.)

MONTHLY DANCE, 1955. The most popular recreational activity at Bainbridge was the monthly recruit dance in a regimental drill hall. Senior companies of recruits hosted recruit WAVES and USO junior hostesses from the area, while USO chaperones, duty officers, and officers with their wives kept a watchful eye. A recruit-dance orchestra provided music, and free refreshments were enjoyed by all. Frequently recruits could also enjoy movies, USO shows, big-name bands, and variety shows at Bainbridge. (*The Compass*, 1955.)

BALTIMORE SYMPHONY ORCHESTRA, 1972. The Center Theatre offered musical delights for naval personnel as well as guests and visitors. Special Services operated the theater seven days a week with matinees on Saturday and Sunday. Among the favorite features were performances by the Baltimore Symphony Orchestra, who took to the stage located in Memorial Hall in the old Tome Area on October 30, 1972. (Courtesy of Rev. George Hipkins.)

NAVY EXCHANGE AND COMMISSARY. The Navy Exchange offered servicemen and family members a wide assortment of goods. The shop was located near the Center Headquarters Building, and the barber and beauty shops, laundry, cobble pick-up station, and Navy Exchange cafeteria could be found nearby. The Commissary Store served as a supermarket to 4,000 families in the 1970s. Manned by civilians and navy personnel, the store's shelves had to be well stocked, especially for payday rushes, when several hundred navy wives invaded the commissary in short order. (The 1970 Unofficial Guide to Bainbridge.)

CHIEF'S CLUB AND ACEY DUCEY, 1970. Dance bands, entertainment, and support of the CPO Mess by some 400-odd chiefs allowed the CPO Club to be remodeled in 1970. The chief's club housed a community bar, dance floors, banquet room, package store, and dining area. The EM and PO Club and Acey Ducey hosted parties and a few "never again" resolutions, according to the 1970 Official Bainbridge Guide Book: "It serves as a meeting place for the intellectual crowd. Topics under continued discussion include women, politics, beer, the Navy, women, world problems, WAVES, beer, religion, women, hot rods, women, etc." (The 1970 Unofficial Guide to Bainbridge.)

BASIE AT FIDDLER'S GREEN, DATE UNKNOWN. The EM Club, which was better known as Fiddler's Green, offered big-name talent several times each year exclusively to enlisted personnel. Every night, dance bands took to the same stage that hosted such notables as Count Basie, photographed here before a packed house. Fiddler's Green also featured a beer bar and a "21" bar, as well as a snack and package store for patrons. (The 1970 Unofficial Guide to Bainbridge.)

OFFICER'S CLUB. A rambling group of buildings that contained a lounge, ballroom, and the O Club Bar, the officer's club also had indoor and outdoor pools, the Monroe Reception Room, a spacious dining room, and self-serve package store. A walnut-paneled club lounge, pictured, was popular for luncheons and evening gatherings. The Monroe Reception Room, as part of the officer's club, was a nod to the building known as the Monroe House during Tome School days. (The 1970 Unofficial Guide to Bainbridge.)

PICNIC AREA, C. 1955. Such a wide-open base with old growth trees and natural water features would necessarily offer opportunities for outdoor activities, including picnics. This was a most popular activity when friends and family visited, especially on Bainbridge Sunday, a tradition at the base. Picnic areas featured barbecues and playgrounds and eventually would offer pavilions constructed by hand on base. The table seen here is laden with delicious home-cooked fare brought from home. (*The Compass*, 1955.)

COMRADES FOR LIFE, 1943. Perhaps the most profound aspect of any military training is the relationships that are forged for life amongst the recruits, as surely was the case for these sailors waving from barracks windows. As reunions were held in 1999 and in subsequent years, veteran men and women returned to Bainbridge and, with laughter and sometimes tears, shared their marching songs and memories. (Library of Congress, Prints and Photographs Division, Gottscho-Schleisner Collection.)

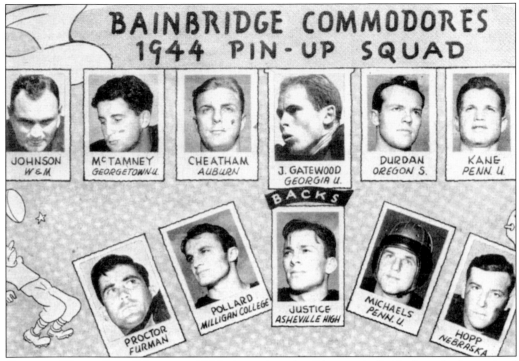

BAINBRIDGE COMMODORES 1944 PIN-UP SQUAD

JOHNSON W&M — MᶜTAMNEY GEORGETOWN U. — CHEATHAM AUBURN — J. GATEWOOD GEORGIA U. — DURDAN OREGON S. — KANE PENN U.

BACKS

PROCTOR FURMAN — POLLARD MILLIGAN COLLEGE — JUSTICE ASHEVILLE HIGH — MICHAELS PENN. U. — HOPP NEBRASKA

CHARLIE "CHOO CHOO" JUSTICE, 1944. A number of well-known individuals worked or trained at Bainbridge, from Willard Scott to Tony Curtis to Bill Cosby to Stan Musial. Gene Tunny was athletics director, and Connie Mack was at Bainbridge scouting. Perhaps one of the greatest football players to ever don a Commodore uniform was Charlie "Choo Choo" Justice, a member of the team in 1944. He was considered by many to be the greatest running back to come from the state of North Carolina. (Courtesy of Mike Miklas.)

OVERSEAS DUTY, UNKNOWN DATE. The majority of men and women who served at NTC Bainbridge did not go on to earn national fame and renown, but they did move on to duty stations across the country and around the world. It is their memories, stories, and photographs that are left to preserve the history of the base. Here Ed Ellison is pictured at one of his duty stations. (Courtesy of Ed Ellison.)

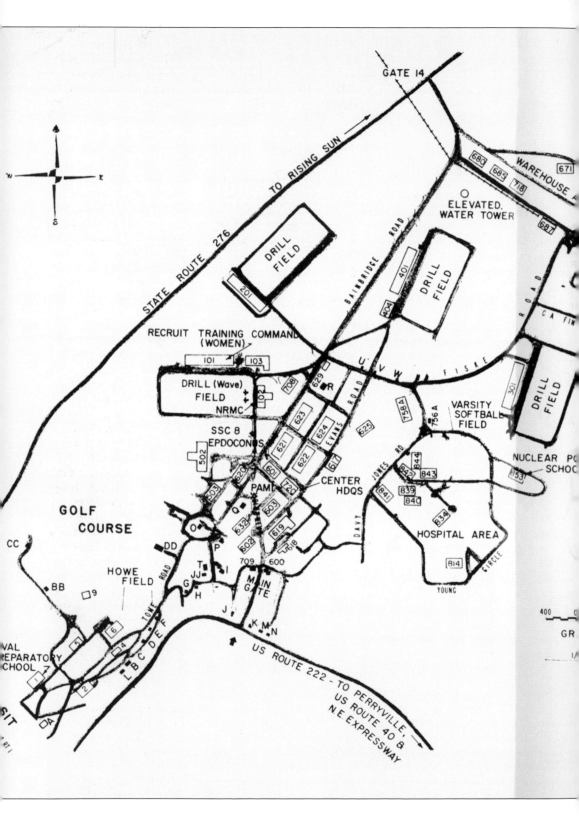

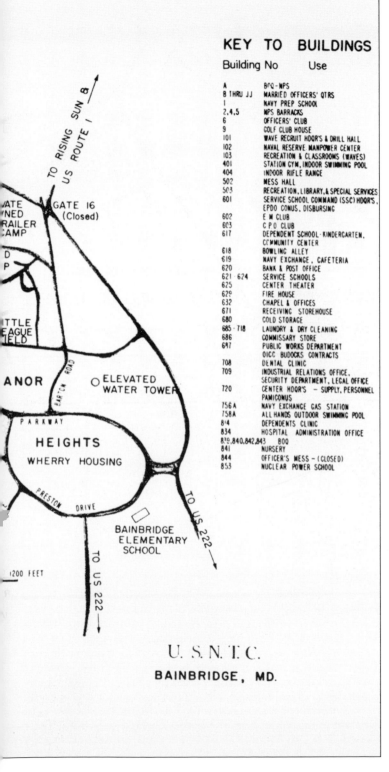

KEY TO BUILDINGS

Building No	Use
A	BOQ-NPS
B THRU JJ	MARRIED OFFICERS' QTRS
I	NAVY PREP SCHOOL
2,4,5	NPS BARRACKS
6	OFFICERS' CLUB
9	GOLF CLUB HOUSE
101	WAVE RECRUIT HDQR'S & DRILL HALL
102	NAVAL RESERVE MANPOWER CENTER
103	RECREATION & CLASSROOMS (WAVES)
401	STATION GYM, INDOOR SWIMMING POOL
404	INDOOR RIFLE RANGE
502	MESS HALL
503	RECREATION, LIBRARY,& SPECIAL SERVICES
601	SERVICE SCHOOL COMMAND (SSC) HDQR'S, EPDO CONUS, DISBURSING
602	E M CLUB
603	C P O CLUB
617	DEPENDENT SCHOOL-KINDERGARTEN, COMMUNITY CENTER
618	BOWLING ALLEY
619	NAVY EXCHANGE, CAFETERIA
620	BANK & POST OFFICE
621-624	SERVICE SCHOOLS
625	CENTER THEATER
629	FIRE HOUSE
632	CHAPEL & OFFICES
671	RECEIVING STOREHOUSE
680	COLD STORAGE
685-718	LAUNDRY & DRY CLEANING
686	COMMISSARY STORE
687	PUBLIC WORKS DEPARTMENT OICC BUDOCKS CONTRACTS
708	DENTAL CLINIC
709	INDUSTRIAL RELATIONS OFFICE, SECURITY DEPARTMENT, LEGAL OFFICE
720	CENTER HDQR'S – SUPPLY, PERSONNEL PAMICONUS
756A	NAVY EXCHANGE GAS STATION
758A	ALL HANDS OUTDOOR SWIMMING POOL
8'4	DEPENDENTS CLINIC
834	HOSPITAL ADMINISTRATION OFFICE
8?9,840,842,843	BOQ
841	NURSERY
844	OFFICER'S MESS – (CLOSED)
853	NUCLEAR POWER SCHOOL

U. S. N. T. C.

BAINBRIDGE, MD.

MAP TO THE BASE, 1970. Bainbridge could be somewhat difficult to navigate, especially because some areas were off-limits and also because others simply weren't visible from one section to another based upon tree lines and topography. Hence updated maps were constant features in guides to Bainbridge, such as the 1970 guide. By that time, however, a number of the buildings were no longer in use. The ones that were had numbers, and their use was clearly defined. Of special interest to most return visitors to Bainbridge is the hospital area featuring the 800 buildings at Young Circle and the nearby Nuclear Power School. Manor Heights and the Wherry Housing area are frequently requested stops on tours, as is the area of the navy-owned and privately owned trailer camps where some local families lived. Between these two areas, notice the Youth Cabin, which was removed to nearby Colora in Cecil County and still serves as a Boy Scout Cabin courtesy of the efforts of Hazel Jenkins. One of the most intact areas of the base in the 21st century is the Recruit Training Command for Women and the WAVE Drill Field, giving visitors some idea of the size and scale of the base. (The 1970 Unofficial Guide to Bainbridge.)

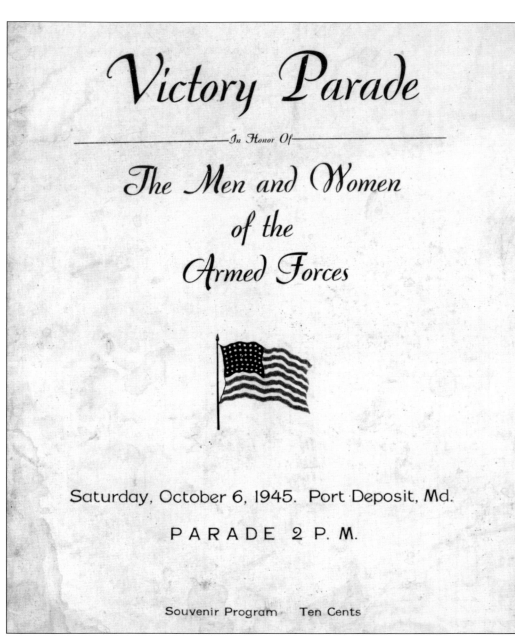

Victory Parade

In Honor Of

The Men and Women
of the
Armed Forces

Saturday, October 6, 1945. Port Deposit, Md.

PARADE 2 P. M.

Souvenir Program   Ten Cents

VICTORY PARADE PROGRAM, 1945. Bainbridge was, essentially, a city unto itself, but the base had an irreversible impact upon agrarian Cecil County and the small riverfront town of Port Deposit especially. Bainbridge personnel were called upon to help during the flood of 1972 in Port Deposit and during a fatal commercial plane crash. They were also called upon to help with celebrations. On October 6, 1945, the town of Port Deposit gave back to the men and women of the armed forces, especially focusing on Bainbridge personnel, when they held a massive Victory Parade and special services throughout the entire town. Souvenir programs quickly sold out of all advertising and then were sold for a dime each to spectators who crowded Main Street and brought bunting and flags to festoon the town in red, white, and blue as they cheered our heroes. These programs are cherished mementos of Port Deposit and Cecil County residents today. (Courtesy of the Paw Paw Museum.)

HOSPITAL GROUP, 1944. The base hospital offered the most up-to-date equipment and techniques in the area during its years of operation and is a frequently requested stop for visitors to the base in the 21st century, primarily because so many children were born there. This photograph, taken at 2,000 feet in August 1944, shows the hospital group just down from the amphitheater. The cause of the thick, black smoke in the upper right-hand corner is unknown. (Department of the Navy, Naval Historical Center.)

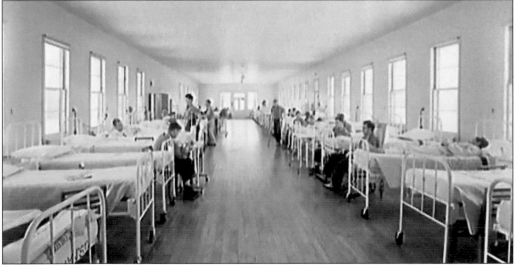

HOSPITAL WARD, 1943. The Bainbridge Hospital Ward, a long, fairly narrow room lined with beds, offered ample natural light through the many windows fitted on both sides of the room. The position of the hospital on base allowed for excellent views of the base by patients recuperating from surgeries or treatments. Bed linens were changed daily and kept crisp and white at the base laundry nearby. (Library of Congress, Prints and Photographs Division, Gottscho-Schleisner Collection)

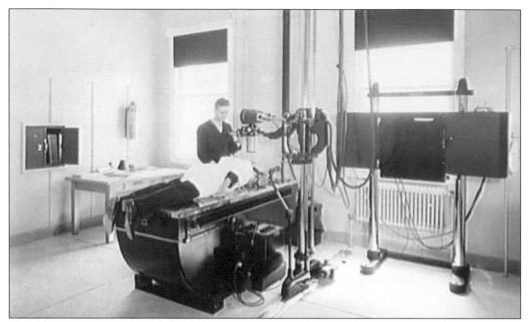

X-RAY ROOM, 1943. Doctors from throughout Cecil and Harford Counties gained an advantage when a modern X-ray room was added to the base hospital, as they were allowed to utilize the facilities when available and necessary, similar to an arrangement made by the Tome School for Boys medical staff in the early part of the century. This model X-ray facility has both a stark and sterile appearance but was a welcome addition to the hospital. (Library of Congress, Prints and Photographs Division, Gottscho-Schleisner Collection.)

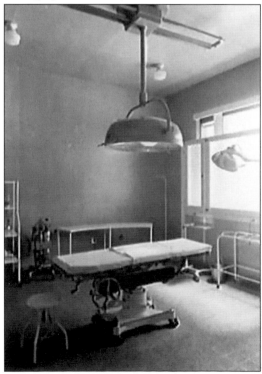

SURGERY FACILITIES, 1943. A neat but fairly sparse surgical room was a centerpiece to the Bainbridge Hospital facilities. Natural light was a primary light source in this surgical suite in the early years, but it was adapted over time. The hospital handled a host of ailments and surgical needs from the routine appendectomy or tonsil surgery to heart surgery. Emergency needs were also met, including stitches after one of those rare pugilistic altercations broken up in quick order by shore patrol. (Library of Congress, Prints and Photographs Division, Gottscho-Schleisner Collection.)

SAILOR'S DINNER, 1943. Normally a crowd of men would join this sailor at his humble picnic table in the mess hall in one of Bainbridge's four regimental areas. But this promotional photograph of 1943 was set up to show the neat, orderly, and healthful conditions of Bainbridge and, in its starkness, is a stirring and dramatic slice of everyday life at Bainbridge. (Library of Congress, Prints and Photographs Division, Gottscho-Schleisner Collection.)

STATUE OF LIBERTY, C. 1943. In a show of American patriotism, men stationed at Bainbridge and the recruits, or "boots," they trained were painstakingly arranged in the shape of Lady Liberty. Other recognizable American symbols, such as an eagle and the Liberty Bell, were created, photographed, and printed on postcards sent home to loved ones across the United States. (U.S. Navy postcard.)

MAIN GATE, C. 1971. This is believed to be the last image of the main gate taken while the base was still relatively well manicured and prior to the erection of the more permanent chain-link fence. The lack of groomed flower beds became a sort of early warning system to locals that the navy might be winding down the base. "It was always pristine—every flower bed, the sidewalks—just not a weed to be seen anywhere," said local resident Jeanette Hillyer, who was known as the "Hello Gal" because she manned the switchboard at Bainbridge. In her later years, she became somewhat of a community activist and worked tirelessly to preserve the memory of NTC Bainbridge. "You could tell it was going to be shut down because things weren't taken care of like they once were, so you just knew what was coming next," she explained. (Courtesy of Kevin Matthews.)

Five

ANCHORS AWAY

Rumors circulated for years in the late 1960s and early 1970s that the days of Bainbridge were numbered. Local residents had borne witness to fickle tides of change over the years, as Bainbridge was sent into caretaker status, mothballed, and reactivated, as well as had new commands brought in, schools added and taken away, and changes wrought. By the 1970s, it appeared the whispered and feared rumor would come to fruition, as the condition of the base continued into rapid deterioration. "Beautiful downtown Bainbridge," became the tongue-in-cheek catchphrase of center personnel when conducting tours showing the base's dilapidated condition, according to the 1973 base newspaper.

Marilyn Pare, a local newspaper reporter in 1974, noted that Bainbridge had become Cecil County's only ghost town and interviewed locals about the final decision to close the base. "Oh, I'll miss it," Ted Duff, a 72-year-old Port Deposit resident told her. Duff was an early recruit at Bainbridge who returned to the base as an officer. "It's hard to believe that March 31 will be the last day."

Starting in the late 1960s and lasting through 1972, schools were gradually closed on base. In May 1972, the last WAVE Company graduated. The last school to close was the Nuclear Power School, which was followed by the closure of the base as a naval training facility in 1976. The base then served as a campus for the federal Job Corps program for 11 years, a time that brought much destruction to the remaining buildings by both vandalism and neglect.

To many local residents, the base became a weed-ridden, abandoned eyesore surrounded by six-foot chain-link fence. To others, it became a forgotten land suitable for poaching, setting fires, and for stealing copper wire and anything else that could turn a quick buck. For all, it became, as Marilyn Pare indicated, a ghost town and a sad legacy. For over 25 years, it would remain in a state of on-again, off-again negotiations for turnover and redevelopment. During that time, the base also underwent asbestos and lead-paint cleanup, became the impetus for economic-development meetings and plans by a reuse committee, and was a constant source of frustration.

THE FLAG COMES DOWN, 1976. Although the date set for the closing of Bainbridge was March 31, final ceremonies were conducted May 31, 1976, with addresses, invocation, special music, a host of spectators, and the dramatic lowering of the flag over NTC Bainbridge. The unkempt condition of the yard and Building 601 in the background is the first minor sign of the neglect and ruin yet to come. (Courtesy of Rev. George Hipkins.)

FOLDING THE FLAG, 1976. Before the benediction, each of the flags that once unfurled proudly over Bainbridge was lowered and folded in solemn order. Veterans, officers, enlisted personnel, local residents, former civilian workers, and local dignitaries attended the sad event, many hoping against hope that something could be done to save the base, and none believing it would fall to rack and ruin in less than a decade. (Courtesy of Rev. George Hipkins.)

OFFICER'S FINAL RETURN, 1976. These three gentlemen returned to Bainbridge to witness the closing ceremonies, all three being naval officers on the base when it opened in 1942. Pictured from left to right are Frank Stipe, William Coyle, and Joseph Fair. They were photographed by the Reverend George Hipkins as the last Bainbridge flag unfurled in a soft chilly breeze in the background. (Courtesy of Rev. George Hipkins.)

CAPTAIN'S ADDRESS, 1976. Captain Wilson offered a brief address to the assembled audience from a dais that was reportedly built in a few short hours the week of the ceremony. The podium was wheeled out from the headquarters building, and chairs were moved over from Building 601. The ceremony, between Building 601 and the Bainbridge Post Office, overlooked St. Paul's Chapel, which was even then beginning to show signs of neglect. (Courtesy of Rev. George Hipkins.)

EASTER TRADITION AT AMPHITHEATER, C. 1976. While the amphitheater was still standing, local residents were determined to continue the tradition of Easter sunrise services in the massive facility. The benches where the men are gathered were for officers, while the backless benches that sprawled up the natural sloping hillside in the foreground were for the enlisted personnel. A navy officer on stage was on hand to supervise. (Courtesy of Rev. George Hipkins.)

GETTING READY FOR EASTER, C. 1976. The Reverend George Hipkins, Port Deposit photographer and pastor emeritus of Port Deposit Presbyterian Church, documented preparations for an Easter sunrise service. While a navy officer was still on hand to supervise, rush cleanup was undertaken at the already deteriorating amphitheater. (Courtesy of Rev. George Hipkins.)

OFFICER AND ENLISTED SEATING, C. 1976. It appears that this bench was being removed from the officer's seating area in preparation for Easter sunrise service and was relocated to the stage of the old amphitheater. The wooden benches fell into terrible disrepair from rot and exposure to the elements once the amphitheater was torn down, but one has been rescued and restored by the Bainbridge Historical Association, and it is displayed in their museum. (Courtesy of Rev. George Hipkins.)

AMPHITHEATER UNDER CONSTRUCTION, C. 1943. It is interesting to compare these two photographs, taken about 33 years apart. This image captures the construction of the massive amphitheater at Bainbridge prior to the rows upon rows of benches and bleachers being added in the natural bowl created by the topography. It took less than three months to build the amphitheater, although only the outline remains today. (Library of Congress, Prints and Photographs Division, Gottscho-Schleisner Collection.)

A Navy and Port Man, 1965. Photographed and interviewed for a 1965 edition of the *Mainsheet*, John E. Schaeffer was stationed at Bainbridge after three and a half years in the Destroyer Navy. He and his wife, Jeannie, purchased a massive old home on Port Deposit's Main Street and became active members of the community, including John's involvement with the NTC Bainbridge Historical Association. (The *Mainsheet*, April 16, 1965.)

Second Regiment, 1978. It may be expected that abandoned buildings would become the victims of vandalism and theft and would begin to show signs of age and neglect fairly quickly. But this aerial photograph from 1978 shows that the second regiment was quickly being taken over by nature, with weeds coming up through the asphalt grinder. The remaining buildings show signs of neglect, but the encroachment of trees and weeds is the real indicator of conditions on base. (Courtesy of Mike Miklas.)

The Mainsheet | **31 years**

Vol. 29 - No. 23   BAINBRIDGE, MARYLAND   June 29, 1973

The Bainbridge heritage
final edition

to remember

With the United States deep into World War Two, Bainbridge opens its doors to a quarter million recruits.

By JO2 Robin Warner and JOSA Steve Chant

Bainbridge's future has been uncertain since first opening its doors in 1942. But the rumors became fact this spring when the Department of Defense announced plans to close the Naval Training Center by 1975.

During its 31-years of existence, the Center has played a major role in the training of Navymen and women; not to mention its contribution toward area economics and civilian employment opportunities.

The history surrounding Bainbridge land is unique. It can be traced back to the days when America still belonged to the Indian.

Until treaties, land grants and political persuasion put the area in the hands of small land owners, Bainbridge was used by the Susquehanna Indians as their hunting grounds.

Unknowingly, one of the area's first settlers played a major part in the establishment of the training Center. The man, Jacob Tome—financier and philanthropist, was Pennsylvania born and poor. At the age of 16 he set out for Port Deposit to make his fortune. Thus, what

began as a one-man logging operation for Tome became an empire.

His small empire also claimed much of Bainbridge's original land. Here, where the Naval Academy Prep School is now located, he established the Jacob Tome Institute for young men and women.

The school survived its originator until 1942, at which time, the Tome preparatory school for boys was sold to the Navy. This, plus 71 adjacent parcels of land from 69 owners, became the 1,132 acres comprising the base.

Construction on Center began April 10, 1942. Contracts were awarded to the Charles R. Tompkins Company of Washington, D.C., providing unlimited job openings for area residents.

Ground breaking operations started May 19 and by Aug. 14, 506 temporary buildings had been constructed. This proved quite an accomplishment, as foul weather, lack of roads, deep mud and an inadequate water supply were enormous obstacles to overcome.

Bainbridge building designs fall into three main architectural classes: Those included in the Tome School purchase are built of field stone representing 19th century architecture. Homes acquired through purchase of individual properties, tend toward modest

contemporary designs. And last are the temporary buildings constructed hurridly to house the upsurge of World War Two.

Most of these Navy buildings, originally designed to withstand 10 years use, remain on Center today, dilapidated and overgrown with foliage.

On Oct. 1, 1942 Bainbridge was commissioned as a naval training station and the first recruit, Damon Sutton of Pittsburgh, Pa., reported aboard Oct. 10. Construction continued through the summer of 1943 where the original contract was fulfilled.

USNTC Bainbridge was named by President Franklin D. Roosevelt in honor of an early naval hero, Commodore William Bainbridge. Commander of the Constitution, a Navy War frigate. Bainbridge was immortalized in the poem "Old Ironsides." He has also been credited with the founding of the Navy's first training school.

Although, Bainbridge was commissioned as a training station in October, its first commanding officer, Commodore C.F. Russell reported aboard for duty in June. He remained in command of the station

See 31 Years, Page Three

THE MAINSHEET REMEMBERED, 1973. Originally called the *Bainbridge Weekly*, the *Mainsheet* became the second largest navy newspaper during the 1940s. It was the brainchild of Capt. C. F. Russell, who called the public-information office at 3:00 p.m. on October 27, 1942, and said, "Let's get a station paper out this Saturday. The boys need something to read over the weekend." The paper documented every facet of Bainbridge's history for 31 years, save the base deactivation following World War II. The first edition didn't come out the Saturday that Captain Russell requested, rather it went to press November 21, 1942, with the name "Mainsheet" coined a month later following a center-wide contest in which the lucky winner received a free phone call home. In 1951, pictures were first seen in the paper, and by 1956, it became one of the navy's largest station tabloids, increasing to 12 pages weekly. In 1968, it was an eight-page biweekly and, in 1970, returned to a weekly layout. The last issue was edited by Robin Warner and appeared June 29, 1973, followed by a weekly newsletter offering the "Center Plan of the Day," from July 6, 1973, until just before the 1976 closing of the base. (The *Mainsheet*, 1973.)

THE TOME SCHOOL, PORT DEPOSIT, MARYLAND

TOME AREA AND PORT DEPOSIT, C. 1905. After the closing of Bainbridge, people were out of work and many moved from the area, if they hadn't already done so in the aftermath of terrible flooding from Tropical Storm Agnes in 1972. No one knew what would happen next, but the tide was starting to turn toward recognizing the history of the area. Following Agnes and in the midst of the base closure procedures, the Port Deposit Heritage Corporation was formed, the basis of the Paw Paw Museum collection was gathered and archived, and the town of Port Deposit was listed on the National Register of Historic Places. Before long, the Tome School for Boys campus was also listed on the National Register. It remains to be seen what will happen to the pastoral landscape in the future. (Courtesy of the author.)

Six

IN REMEMBRANCE AND HONOR

The condition of the former NTC Bainbridge during the 1970s was a sad testament to the legacy of the men and women of the "greatest generation" who founded the base and of those that followed. Even prior to the official closing ceremonies in 1976, large-scale destruction, deterioration, and vandalism could be observed in any out-of-the-way corner of the base that was for the most part not monitored by anyone on base.

Following the official closing exercises, the Job Corps moved in, as did trespassers ignoring the posted no-trespassing signs, and decay and deterioration moved at a much quicker pace. Because the base structures were primarily temporary when built, most contained lead paint, asbestos, and other environmental hazards and issues, meaning bulldozers and other heavy equipment were brought in to tear down most of what remained.

During this time, however, groups formed and united to preserve the history and legacy of Bainbridge, clean up the base, and hold reunions.

MAIN GATE ENTRANCE, 2007. The former main gate entrance off Route 222 was one of the first sights a new recruit had of Bainbridge, and it stuck in their memory for years to come. Since most returning veterans to the base sought out the main gate, its demolition was particularly painful. All that remains is a crumbling concrete curb where the guard box stood, the barest outline of building foundations, and a ruined sidewalk. (Courtesy of Kevin Matthews.)

SIGN OF REMEMBERING, 2000. Photographed the morning of the transfer ceremony, February 14, 2000, this sign was at the old main gate for veterans returning to the base. Paul Fleming, Mike Miklas, and Porter May were early organizers of the Bainbridge Reunion Association to memorialize the 31-year legacy of the facility. The sign is on the chain-link fence with the guard-box curb behind it and Bainbridge Road in the background. (Courtesy of Kevin Matthews.)

MOTHBALLED BARRACKS, C. 1970. Although sections of the base had already been reduced to inactivity, or mothballed, some of the abandoned barracks appeared ready to accept recruits on a moment's notice with lockers and bunks neatly lined up and the room hall still clean. Mike Miklas, who shot this picture, still greatly regrets not saving the lockers and bunks from the wrecking ball and their eventual burial on base. (Courtesy of Mike Miklas.)

ABANDONED BARRACKS, C. 1973. Mike Miklas trained his camera on the same barracks a handful of years later to record the quick destruction of the same scene. By then, all of the bunks had been removed or stolen, the lockers toppled and damaged, and interior finishes containing asbestos removed. This shot was taken just days before the wrecking ball wiped this building out. (Courtesy of Mike Miklas.)

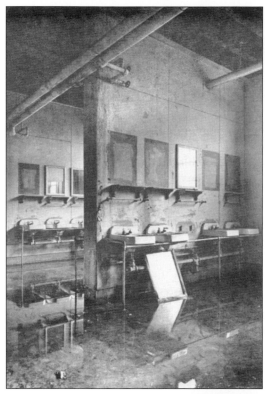

FOURTH REGIMENT BARRACKS, 1975. Photographed by Paul Hutchins for *The Sun* magazine edition of June 8, 1975, the ruination of Bainbridge was clearly evident in the 4th Regiment barracks. Missing mirrors, broken windows, and water from broken pipes and leaking roofs were common. A missing sink and cast-off mirror were stark evidence of wanton vandalism and theft occurring even then. (*The Sun* magazine, the *Baltimore Sun*, June 8, 1975.)

MESS HALL, 1975. Where once tables were lined up in military order and recruits scrubbed floors to a shine, by 1975, there was nothing but a mess in the old mess or chow hall. Overturned and broken tables, shattered light fixtures and windows, and graffiti were stark evidence that the building's ruinous condition was not the result of neglect alone but of vandalism as well. (*The Sun* magazine, the *Baltimore Sun*, June 8, 1975.)

98

BOWLING ALLEY, 1975. Once a popular spot for fun, the Bainbridge Bowling Alley was quickly reduced to ruin. Wood alleys were, allegedly, ripped out for hardwood flooring by a light-fingered do-it-yourselfer. The tree limbs were the result of a gaping hole in the roof. Pins, balls, chairs, tables, and signage were the first items stolen when the building was abandoned. (*The Sun* magazine, the *Baltimore Sun*, June 8, 1975.)

KITCHEN, 1975. Where once massive meals were prepared and served, peeling paint, filth, ruin, and debris reigned by 1975. The base was still open when this photograph was taken, but this kitchen was no longer in use and therefore was allowed to rot. In the background are the gleaming kettles ready to use, simply left behind when this section of Bainbridge was abandoned. (*The Sun* magazine, the *Baltimore Sun*, June 8, 1975.)

DRILL FIELD, 1988. When veterans Al Bagley and Mike Miklas flew over Bainbridge in 1988, this was the view awaiting them, which wasn't visible from vistas outside the fence. The drill field was returning to nature, and the encroaching vegetation had all but consumed even the largest of buildings left standing. "This was what remained of the Bainbridge I knew," Miklas recalled. "We had to do something." (Courtesy of Mike Miklas.)

AERIAL OF BASE, 1943. This 1943 aerial shot, taken from 10,000 feet courtesy of an airplane on loan from Norfolk, shows the stark contrast of the base as seen from above. All four regimental drill fields, or grinders, are visible, along with the amphitheater near the center. (Department of the Navy, Naval Historical Center.)

SECOND REGIMENT, 1943. A more detailed shot of the 2nd Regiment drill field, taken that same day in 1943 at an altitude of 700 feet, shows the manicured condition of the base, even as old-growth trees were left standing and new landscaping added to the still dusty, unpaved base. Wooden sidewalks had been placed in officer areas due to dust and mud to keep things tidy. (Department of the Navy, Naval Historical Center.)

TOME SCHOOL AREA, 1999. Seen from the air, the Tome School area, or NAPS (Naval Academy Preparatory School), at the former NTC Bainbridge still shows signs of an attractive appearance. Closer inspection shows boarded-up windows, as the base awaits a reuse decision for the property. This photograph was taken after volunteer cleanups had been occurring every Saturday from May through October since 1997. (Courtesy of Mike Miklas.)

HARRISON HOUSE, 1998. This structure was condemned after thieves removed copper gutters, causing leaks and structural instability. During the Tome School Clean-Up Volunteers projects, all debris surrounding this building was removed, but by 2001, the structure had again been attacked by vandals who camped in one room with a barbecue for warmth as they chipped away at architectural details, including a hand-carved fireplace mantle that featured the Tome School logo. (Courtesy of the author.)

MADISON HOUSE, 1998. This former Tome School for Boys dormitory sits on the interior of the campus between the powerhouse and Memorial Hall and was one of the least damaged. The navy removed the side porches of the granite structure to add air-conditioning units and fire escapes, giving it a more nondescript appearance, which may have kept treasure hunters at bay and thus spared the building significant abuse. (Courtesy of the author.)

MONROE HOUSE GYMNASIUM, 1998. The weeds and trees in the foreground are growing through dirt, filling the former navy pool beside this building, which housed the officer's club and the Monroe Room reception hall. The large building with broken-out windows was the gymnasium, beside it was the indoor pool, and the front of the building was the Monroe House, which served the navy as a club, game room, and lounge. (Courtesy of the author.)

MONROE HOUSE, 1998. The original granite portion of this building was built about 1901 and served as the cafeteria before becoming a theater and gym for the Tome School for Boys. The barely visible sign between the pillars indicates that the building, like others, had been condemned and was in danger of collapse. By 2001, part of the sign's prediction came true, when the roof collapsed into the indoor pool. (Courtesy of the author.)

VAN BUREN HOUSE, 1998. This building, which once welcomed Franklin Delano Roosevelt as a guest speaker to Tome, was in deplorable condition by the mid-1990s. The rear cafeteria and kitchens gave the appearance of a haunted house ready for a horror-movie crew. Visible from Route 222, most of the wood trim on both the interior and exterior was removed by thieves over the course of about 10 years. (Courtesy of the author.)

MEMORIAL HALL, 1998. Its clock covered by plywood, the tower of Memorial Hall retained its original copper because it was too difficult for thieves to reach. However, this is the last known picture of the quill weather vane, as it was stolen in 1999. Any place where copper could easily be reached was stripped; the columns are half painted white to cover graffiti, while one of the three doors shows signs of another break-in. (Courtesy of the author.)

HUNTER HALL, 1998. One of a handful of navy buildings standing, Hunter Hall holds a commanding view of the countryside on a hill along Route 222. The guardian of the hillside created by the wrecked debris of the other buried Bainbridge buildings, this building and environs offer the best glimpse at the size and scope of each regiment, as the drill-hall foundation, chow hall, and grinder can still be identified by visitors. (Courtesy of the author.)

FLEET RESERVE BAINBRIDGE MEMORIAL DEDICATION, 1993. Navy veterans and Bainbridge were remembered in everlasting granite, even as Bainbridge crumbled atop the hill in 1993. The Bainbridge Fleet Reserve, Branch 168, placed and dedicated a memorial to NTC Bainbridge on October 13, 1993, Navy Day. All pomp and circumstance surrounded the day. (Courtesy of Rev. George Hipkins.)

HONOR GUARD, 1993. A Bainbridge Memorial was dedicated by Bainbridge Fleet Reserve Association (FRA) in 1993 in Port Deposit's Marina Park. The Perryville American Legion Honor Guard was on hand to support the event, as were members of the Port Deposit VFW Jerry Skrivanek Post No. 8185 and dozens of U.S. Navy veterans and town residents. The FRA took the lead in memorializing Bainbridge. (Courtesy of Rev. George Hipkins.)

VETERANS MEMORIAL, 1992. A year prior to dedication of the Bainbridge Memorial, Port Deposit VFW Jerry Skrivanek Post No. 8185 dedicated a memorial to all the men and women of the community who served in the military. This monument, also of granite, was located in Marina Park along the Susquehanna River shore in Port Deposit, where once navy sailors visited boat docks and participated in boat drills in the river behind this monument. (Courtesy of Rev. George Hipkins.)

TOME SCHOOL CLEAN-UP VOLUNTEERS. In 1997, through the initiative of Delegate David Rudolph, a group of volunteers were organized through Port Deposit Heritage Corporation's president Glen Longacre, Judy Leonard, and the author. Pictured on the steps of Monroe Hall is a small group of the dedicated volunteers who worked every Saturday from May through October from 1997 until the transfer of the base on February 14, 2000. (Courtesy of the author.)

DELEGATE DAVID RUDOLPH, 1997. An educator and Maryland delegate, David Rudolph inspired creation of the Tome School Clean-Up Volunteers and was a frequent visitor to the cleanups, pitching in when not in session at Annapolis, to chip away at years of debris. Here Rudolph and co-organizer Erika Quesenbery, author of this book, plan the work to be accomplished during a cleanup in mid-November 1998. (Courtesy of the Paw Paw Museum.)

MONROE HOUSE, BEFORE, 1998. Shot from the quad in front of Monroe House, this photograph shows the debris and dead trees that surrounded Monroe House on October 17, 1998, when the volunteers moved from the headmaster's house to Monroe to begin cleanup efforts there. The granite steps to the front of this building were quite literally impassable, as so much multiflora rose had accumulated on the steps as to block them entirely from use. (Courtesy of the author.)

MONROE HOUSE, AFTER, 1998. Just two weeks later, the multiflora rose and dead trees were removed and years of brush growth and rotted plant material were swept away, revealing a handsome granite structure. Tome School Clean-Up Volunteers accomplished this feat using hand tools from home and a rented weed whacker. When the weeds were removed from the buildings, original signposts for each structure were found near the steps. (Courtesy of the author.)

HEADMASTER'S HOUSE, BEFORE, 1998. One of the most significantly damaged buildings in the Tome Area was the headmaster's house, which was the first building abandoned. Massive trees had literally overtaken the property, blocking any view of the structure from any of the other buildings. The interior was gutted of anything of value, and that which had no value was destroyed for no reason whatsoever. (Courtesy of the author.)

HEADMASTER'S HOUSE, AFTER, 1998. After a full day of removing dead trees, limbs, and debris, the Tome School Clean-Up Volunteers completely cleared the front of the building and exposed it to much-needed light and drying out for the first time in over a quarter century. Because of rampant deterioration, it was the first structure tackled by Paul Risk Associates in 2006 for stabilization. (Courtesy of the author.)

SEN. ROBERT HOOPER, 1998. Seeing pictures of how the headmaster's house once looked and of the degradation of the structure sent volunteers into overdrive to remove an encroaching woods with one chain saw and hand-held garden tools. Members of the Broomell family of Colora, at left, were constant volunteers, as was Sen. Robert Hooper of Harford County, seen here heading for first aid after losing a battle with a branch. (Courtesy of the author.)

THE QUAD, 1998. Kate McCauley of Lancaster County, Pennsylvania, made the journey to the Tome area to lend a hand in the cleanup efforts. Local farmers, including Glen Longacre, Edwin Merriman, and Harry Hepbron, donated use of their farm equipment to the project, enabling volunteers to cut back weeds and grass on the practice quad and football field. (Courtesy of the author.)

JOHN BUCK, 1998. Cleanup volunteers came from all walks of life and areas of the country, from Maryland and Pennsylvania, to Nebraska, South Carolina, and Florida. Among the volunteers was John Buck, attorney for the town of Port Deposit and son of Judge Walter Buck, a graduate of the Tome School for Boys. John brought a very welcome chain saw for the scrub forest at the headmaster's house. (Courtesy of the author.)

JUDGE WALTER BUCK, 1998. The Tome School volunteers received inspiration and motivation when Judge Walter Buck, one of the last graduates of the Tome School for Boys and a Bainbridge Re-Use Advisory Committee member, visited the cleanup site on campus with his high school yearbook. He shared his stories of campus life and how well the grounds were once maintained. (Courtesy of the author.)

HYDRANT IN ITALIAN GARDENS, 1998. Dry fire hydrants that had been rusting for a decade were cleared of debris, poison ivy, overgrowth and miles of vines by volunteers during the cleanup project. Here L. Ray Quesenbery Jr., a retired mail carrier from Fallston in Harford County, Maryland, and father of the author, wins the battle with a particularly aggressive poison sumac that had claimed this hydrant in the Italian Gardens. (Courtesy of the author.)

ITALIAN GARDENS, 1998. The gardens were known to be in front of Memorial Hall, past the roadway, but years of overgrowth obscured them from view. Granite steps were covered with earth and leaves that had become compost, while balustrades were torn apart by vandals. Once the original ornamental trees and gardens were found, they were quickly cleared of vines by such volunteers as Ann Quesenbery, mother of the author. (Courtesy of the author.)

GARDEN STEPS, 1998. Nearly four feet of debris was removed by volunteers Kevin Matthews and the author before this set of steps, the first in a double series of steps to the Italian Gardens, were unearthed. Made of dressed Port Deposit granite, the railing had long since been stolen, and the concrete bases to iron lamp posts had been destroyed in order for thieves to make off with all the light fixtures, save one lamp hidden in the debris. (Courtesy of Ann Quesenbery.)

QUARTERS C, 1998. Derelict structures designed by the top architects of their day as housing for the prestigious Tome School instructors and later used as officer housing at NAPS also fell prey to vandalism and neglect. Quarters C, with windows that follow the line of the interior stairs, was rescued from vegetation by the cleanup volunteers. (Courtesy of the author.)

TRANSFER CEREMONY, 2000. After years of cleanup by volunteers and Seabees, the navy held one final ceremony at the base on February 14, 2000, under a large tent that was erected in the parking lot for the main gate. The tent was filled to capacity with naval and civilian personnel, elected officials, and invited guests to witness the historic event. (Courtesy of Mike Miklas.)

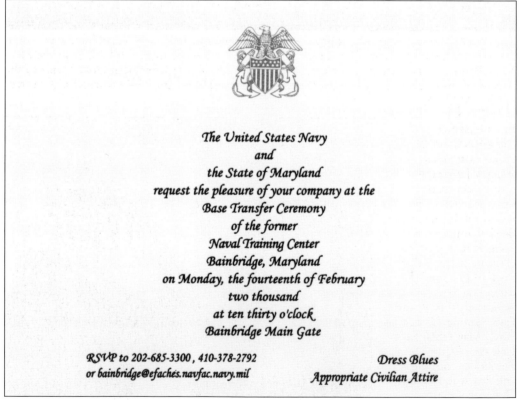

The United States Navy
and
the State of Maryland
request the pleasure of your company at the
Base Transfer Ceremony
of the former
Naval Training Center
Bainbridge, Maryland
on Monday, the fourteenth of February
two thousand
at ten thirty o'clock
Bainbridge Main Gate

RSVP to 202-685-3300 , 410-378-2792   *Dress Blues*
or bainbridge@efaches.navfac.navy.mil   *Appropriate Civilian Attire*

INVITATION TO TRANSFER, 2000. This invitation was distributed by the navy for the final transfer ceremony, which would bring to an end the beleaguered abandonment of Bainbridge. Held at the main gate under a massive tent, the event was held on Valentine's Day, February 14, 2000, with then Lt. Comdr. Jeff Borowy, the last commander of Bainbridge at the transfer, organizing the event with others, including Judy Leonard of the Port Deposit Heritage Corporation and a cleanup volunteer. (Courtesy of the author.)

TRANSFER CEREMONY, 2000. Unlike the closing ceremonies held in 1976, cold and rain moved transfer ceremonies under a large tent. Guests enjoyed music from the U.S. Atlantic Fleet Navy Band and the Advance of the Colors by the U.S. Navy Ceremonial Guard prior to the signing of the Ceremonial Deed. At the podium, Mike Miklas gave the invocation. (Courtesy of Mike Miklas.)

FLAG-PASSING CEREMONY, 2000. One of the most moving tributes during the transfer ceremony was the ceremonial passing of the American flag beginning with Tome School for Boys graduate Judge Walter Buck III (left) and extending to navy personnel Al Bagley and Paul Fleming; Comdr. Porter May, USN, Ret.; Paul Arnold, former Bainbridge caretaker; and finally to Harland Graef, chairperson of the newly created Bainbridge Development Corporation. (Courtesy of the *Rising Sun Herald*.)

CEREMONIAL DEED, 2000. Assistant Secretary of the U.S. Navy Robert B. Pirie and U.S. Sen. Paul S. Sarbanes flank the ceremonial deed signed by themselves and six others at the transfer ceremony. Other signers included Congressman Wayne T. Gilchest; Gene Lynch from then-governor Parris Glendening's staff; and Harland Graef, chairman of the newly formed Bainbridge Development Corporation. (Courtesy of Mike Miklas.)

FINAL TRIBUTES, 2000. The last commander of Bainbridge, Lt. Comdr. Jeff Borowy (left), honored the hard work and dedication of Delegate David Rudolph, who was instrumental in the turnover of the old navy base and in instituting necessary cleanups to facilitate the final transfer ceremony. Years later, in 2006, Captain Borowy returned to the base to take a tour of the facility with Rudolph. (Courtesy of Mike Miklas.)

SIGNING THE CONTRACT, 2000. Prior to the transfer ceremony, a less formal and far less public event took place in the Cecil County Courthouse in Elkton, Maryland. It was here that Lt. Comdr. Jeff Borowy, USN, and Harland Graef (left), chairman of the Bainbridge Development Corporation, signed the official documents to transfer the former USNTC Bainbridge to the State of Maryland for redevelopment by Graef's organization. (Courtesy of the *Rising Sun Herald.*)

REUNION TOUR, 1999. Prior to turnover of the base, veterans banded together to remember Bainbridge and hold a reunion with bus tours of the base, a luncheon on the recently cleared quad in the Tome School area, and even a flyover courtesy of a helicopter. One of the popular tour guides for the event was Al Bagley of Havre de Grace, Maryland, who boarded a helicopter for some aerial photographs. (Courtesy of Mike Miklas.)

BAINBRIDGE MUSEUM, 2007. The Bainbridge Historical Association envisions having a complete museum built on the base and has received the promise of a donation of land from the Bainbridge Development Corporation to bring this dream to a reality. Currently the museum is housed in rented quarters on Port Deposit's Main Street alongside the Port Side Grille restaurant and the Susquehanna River. (Courtesy of Kevin Matthews.)

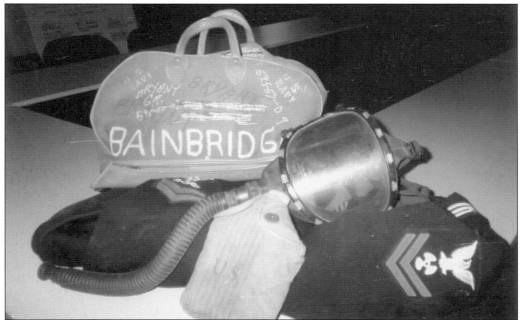

BAINBRIDGE MEMORABILIA, 2007. Port Deposit Heritage Corporation members have been collecting and preserving items from Bainbridge for years, including uniforms, a canteen, and even one of the gas masks distributed on base. The complete gas mask and bag, marked Bainbridge, were donated by town resident Maggie Jackson and displayed at the Paw Paw Museum. (Courtesy of the author.)

LAST FLAG, 2007. Donated by Harland Graef, first chairman of the Bainbridge Development Corporation, this flag was the last in use at NTC Bainbridge and was part of the flag-passing ceremony during the turnover of the base in 2000. It is preserved under glass and on permanent display at the Paw Paw Museum in Port Deposit. (Courtesy of the author.)

CEREMONIAL DEED

THE UNITED STATES OF AMERICA, acting by and through the Department of the Navy, hereby transfers all right, title and interest in the former NAVAL TRAINING CENTER BAINBRIDGE, to the STATE OF MARYLAND acting by and through the Bainbridge Development Corporation on this date, February 14, 2000.

ROBERT B. PIRIE
ASSISTANT SECRETARY OF THE NAVY
(INSTALLATIONS & ENVIRONMENT)

PAUL S. SARBANES
U.S. SENATE

GENE LYNCH
DEPUTY CHIEF OF STAFF, GOVERNOR
OF THE STATE OF MARYLAND

MICHAEL R. JOHNSON
REAR ADMIRAL, CEC, U.S. NAVY

WAYNE T. GILCHREST
U.S. HOUSE OF REPRESENTATIVES

HARLAND GRAEF
CHAIRMAN, BAINBRIDGE
DEVELOPMENT CORPORATION

PAUL G. McMAHON, JR.
CAPTAIN, CEC, U.S. NAVY

BRADLEY CAMPBELL
ADMINISTRATOR, EPA REGION III

CEREMONIAL DEED, 2007. The large ceremonial deed used during the February 14, 2000, turnover ceremony of the Bainbridge Naval Base from federal property to the State of Maryland has been preserved at the Paw Paw Museum. Bearing the signatures of dignitaries, such as U.S. Sen. Paul Sarbanes and Congressman Wayne T. Gilchrest, it is on permanent display at the museum. (Courtesy of the author.)

Jetty Restored, 2007. Among the recent improvements to Port Deposit is the restoration of the jetty, complete with plans for a veterans' plaza and installation of an informational kiosk of the area's military history. The jetty is on the town's waterfront, where once the navy boat docks stood and where long boats were used for training on the Susquehanna River. (Courtesy of the author.)

Main Entrance Sign, 2007. Using the old sign that once welcomed new recruits, developers of the old navy base declare the changes to come to the long-abandoned property. Plans in 2007 include a continuous-care facility in the Tome Area as well as a housing development/mixed-use community, complete with an industrial/commercial component that would return jobs to the area. (Courtesy of the author.)

BAINBRIDGE FENCE, 2007. Although plans for redevelopment of the base are moving ahead, the chain-link fence surrounding the property offers little barrier to trespassers who ignore posted signs. Near Quarters K, a fresh hole was cut in the fence immediately under a no-trespassing sign to gain access to ramshackle structures that are already stripped of any past glories. (Courtesy of the author.)

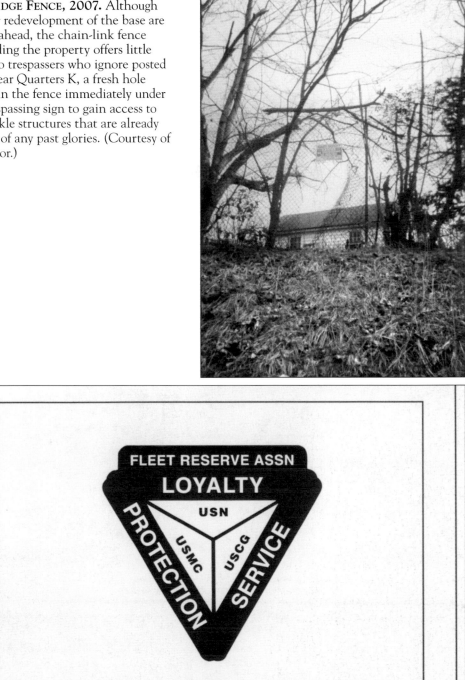

FLEET RESERVE LOGO. This logo of the Fleet Reserve Association, provided by Ed Ellison, is on a small postcard featuring the logo on one side and the preamble to the constitution of the Fleet Reserve Association on the reverse, noting the FRA is "ever mindful of the glorious traditions of the U.S. Navy Marine Corps and Coast Guard." (Courtesy of Ed Ellison.)

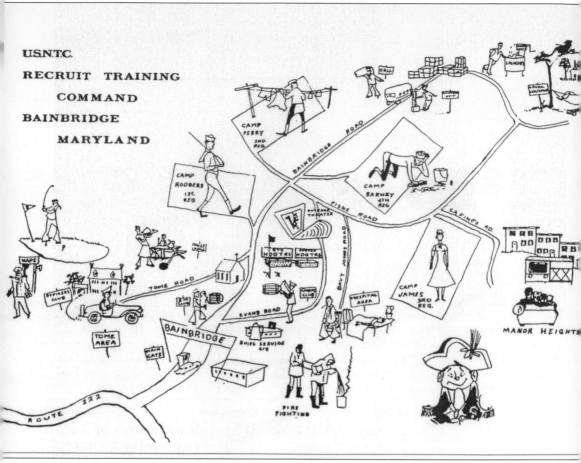

HAND-DRAWN MAP OF BAINBRIDGE, 1950s. This map, hand-drawn and once featured in Bainbridge guidebooks, is now a treasured memento, frequently copied from books and framed by veterans. It is interesting to observe the differences in the base over time, including the location of women in Camp James, 3rd Regiment, prior to the location of WAVES in the 1st Regiment, Camp Rodgers. Camp Perry in the 3rd Regiment is noted with those guarded clotheslines, while a weary sailor scrubs the deck at Camp Barney in the 4th Regiment. Also featured are the location of the outdoor theater, hospital area, old firefighting area, ships-service building, and of course the main gate. Manor Heights is to the right, above the caricature of Commodore William Bainbridge. (Courtesy of Ed Ellison.)

NTC Bainbridge Reunion, 1999. Both neighbors to Bainbridge, Jeanette Hillyer and Cliff Brubaker were active planners and participants in the first Bainbridge reunion. Hillyer was recruited to be the "Hello Gal" at Bainbridge, a civilian working the switchboard. Brubaker lives near Gate 16 currently and was a chief gunners mate and company commander at Bainbridge until 1947, when he transferred to Great Lakes, Illinois. (Courtesy of Mike Miklas.)

NTC Bainbridge Reunion Picnic, 1999. Hundreds returned to Bainbridge base for the first reunion in 1999, hoping to rekindle memories on a guided bus tour. Since most of the buildings had been demolished and the grounds overgrown, pictures of yesteryear were passed around to ignite memories and start the stories flowing. (Courtesy of the *Rising Sun Herald*.)

30 - The Herald — **Neighbors** — The week of October 4, 1999

Sailors unite over bittersweet memories on base

Continued from Front Page

men were trained in the U.S. Navy.

A commemorative booklet, featuring pictures of grinders, drill halls, chow halls, the commissary, stores, Fiddlers Green, the chapel and much more, were sold on Thursday.

During the three-day participants could look at pictures which matched numbered stops along the extensive three-hour tour of the base. Ten motorcoaches transported participants back in time as misty eyed men and women stepped onto the drill fields where they trained, some for the first time in over 50 years.

"It is all so overwhelming to remember the way it was and see how it is now," said former Commander of PAMI CONUS at Bainbridge W.R. Squire of Wilmington, Del. "It is difficult to picture it the way it was but that doesn't stop the memories."

Although for most of the reunion attendees the familiar barracks where they stayed are long since gone. But for Squire he and his daughter, Cynthia, were able to see the house they lived in at Bainbridge. Squire and his family lived in Quarters C, located on the old Tome School for Boys campus as a former Master's Cottage.

Orville March of Newark,

Del., was possibly one of the longest serving on the reunion. He pulled multiple tours, from boot to civilian service. "I can't believe all that went into making this tour a success," March of Newark, Del, said. "There's a lot of teary eyes on this base today."

Charles M. Rutter of Lancaster, Pa., also took the tour of Bainbridge. Rutter was stationed at USNTC Bainbridge in 1943, in the first years in which the base was active. "There's nothing left of what I remember, but just being back here I remember so much," he said. "You never forget."

One participant brought along a copy of his Cruise yearbook from 1956 and pointed out the photograph of Willard Scott who went through training with him at Regiment Four. "He looks a lot different now, he was about 100 pounds lighter then," Rutter noticed.

"We were all about 100 pounds lighter back then," responded March.

Bill Dilling of Ceciton also made the trek to Bainbridge to see the few remnants and relics of a base that once housed 38,000 boots at its peak. "It was something," Dilling said, "you can look at it now, and look at the pictures, but you can't ever imagine what it really was. It was just something you can't describe or rebuild."

> "There's a lot of teary eyes on this base today."
> - Orville March
> USNTC Bainbridge

ALL PHOTOS BY: ERIKA QUESENBERY, HERALD EDITOR

Whether in the same regiment or not, even years of service didn't matter, as reunion attendees shared pictures, stories and tears while on base last Friday.

At left, former Commander of PAMI CONUS W. Squires poses with his daughter Cynthia. The Squires family lived on base in Quarters C, which is still standing on the Tome School for Boys campus. They were one of the few visitors who were actually able to see a building they lived in while on base. Cynthia and her sisters have also vowed to write down and share their favorite memories of the horse stables and beautiful trail rides at USNTC Bainbridge.

MEMORIAL HALL CLOCK TOWER, 2006. The Bainbridge Development Corporation signed an agreement with Manekin, LLC, and Paul Risk Associates in 2006 to begin redevelopment of Bainbridge. The latter company, with offices in Quarryville, Pennsylvania, and in Port Deposit, Maryland, agreed to tackle the stabilization and eventual adaptive reuse of the old Tome School for Boys campus, which is listed on the National Register of Historic Places. (Courtesy of Paul Risk Associates.)

HEADMASTER'S HOUSE STABILIZATION, 2006. Under the experienced guidance of Paul Risk Associates, the buildings of the former Tome School for Boys are coming back to life from a long and destructive slumber. The headmaster's house was one of the first buildings the company began work on to stabilize the roof and support the failing porch after columns had rotted through. (Courtesy of Paul Risk Associates.)

MADISON HOUSE STABILIZATION, 2006. One of the lesser buildings in size, Madison House was used during the final navy cleanup in 1996–1997 to store lumber and tools for their daunting project. After installing temporary scaffolding around the perimeter of the building, Paul Risk Associates began stabilization efforts for the building in 2006 with an eye for resurrecting the campus as a continuous-care facility in the future. (Courtesy of Paul Risk Associates.)

MONROE HOUSE STABILIZATION, 2006. Efforts to stabilize the roof of Monroe House were temporarily put on hold when layer after layer of roofing material were discovered underneath temporary plastic sheeting placed over the roof by the navy in the late 1990s. As a National Register of Historic Places property, research was required to determine the original roofing material used on the structure before stabilization could continue. (Courtesy of Paul Risk Associates.)

BOAT DRILL, C. 1944. Days of white-suited sailors on the Susquehanna are past, but the 2006–2007 restoration of the old jetty in Port Deposit's Marina Park is aiding in securing the navy legacy. A memorial plaza for veterans with an informational kiosk is also planned through the efforts of the Lower Susquehanna Heritage Greenway and local volunteers John Klisavage and Jeanette Hillyer of Port Deposit. (Courtesy of the author.)

DRILL FIELD REVIEW, C. 1969. Bainbridge will never again see the days of dress whites and flags snapping in the breeze in front of dignitaries lining the drill field, or grinder. But a new chapter has opened for Bainbridge, and with the help of organizations such as the Bainbridge Historical Association and Port Deposit Heritage Corporation's Paw Paw Museum, the memories of these days gone by shall be preserved. (The 1970 Unofficial Guide to Bainbridge.)

MIKE MIKLAS, 1951. A shield-styled sign is cut off on the right of this photograph. Mike Miklas is pictured here in uniform in 1951 at Bainbridge. His continued passion for the preservation of Bainbridge's history has kept him preserving and acquiring Bainbridge ephemera, conducting tours, and leading the Bainbridge Historical Association well into his 70s. Miklas met his wife, Jeanette, at Bainbridge and is one of the few people who can successfully navigate the weed-ridden base, pointing out former building locations by both number and function without aid of maps or logs. To Mike and his comrades, we hope for "Fair Winds and Following Seas." (Courtesy of Mike Miklas.)

ACROSS AMERICA, PEOPLE ARE DISCOVERING SOMETHING WONDERFUL. *THEIR HERITAGE.*

Arcadia Publishing is the leading local history publisher in the United States. With more than 3,000 titles in print and hundreds of new titles released every year, Arcadia has extensive specialized experience chronicling the history of communities and celebrating America's hidden stories, bringing to life the people, places, and events from the past. To discover the history of other communities across the nation, please visit:

www.arcadiapublishing.com

Customized search tools allow you to find regional history books about the town where you grew up, the cities where your friends and family live, the town where your parents met, or even that retirement spot you've been dreaming about.